THE CHRISTIAN FAMILY

CONTRIBUTORS

Dr John Habgood retired in 1995 as Archbishop of York. He is a noted writer on theological issues particularly in the field of science and religion.

Dr Grace Jantzen is John Rylands Senior Research Fellow at the University of Manchester. Her work on feminist and ecological theology and on medical ethics is widely respected.

Dr Alistair McFadyen lectures in Systematic Theology at the University of Leeds. He is currently engaged in a major work on the doctrine of sin which includes a study of child abuse.

Dr Alistair Mason lectures in Church History at the University of Leeds. He has a special interest in nineteenth century religion in Britain and America.

Dr Hugh Pyper lectures in Old Testament Studies and Hebrew at the University of Leeds. He has published on the literary study of the Bible and Kierkegaard.

Professor Gerard Rochford was Professor of Social Work Studies in the University of Aberdeen. He has published, *inter alia*, on bereavement and the ethics of psychological experimentation.

Dr Jacqui Stewart lectures in theology at the University of Leeds. She has also taught in the Genetics department and maintains a concern for issues in medical ethics.

Professor Haddon Willmer holds the chair of Theology and Religious Studies in the University of Leeds. He is particularly known for his writings on political theology.

Professor Frances Young is Dean of the Faculty of Arts in the University of Birmingham. Her many books include studies of aspects of the New Testament and the early church.

THE CHRISTIAN FAMILY

– a concept in crisis

edited by
HUGH PYPER

The Canterbury Press
Norwich

© Hugh S. Pyper and the Contributors 1996

First published 1996 by The Canterbury Press Norwich
(a publishing imprint of Hymns Ancient & Modern Limited,
a registered charity)
St Mary's Works, St Mary's Plain,
Norwich, Norfolk, NR3 3BH

British Library Cataloguing in Publication Data

A catalogue record for this book is available
from the British Library

ISBN 1-85311-124-4

*Typeset by Rowland Phototypesetting Ltd,
Bury St Edmunds, Suffolk and
Printed and bound in Great Britain by
St Edmundsbury Press Ltd,
Bury St Edmunds, Suffolk*

CONTENTS

Preface   *page* vii

1 **The Family and the New Social Order**   1
   Dr John Habgood

2 **The Family in the Biblical Tradition**   14
   Dr Hugh Pyper

3 **The Family in the Early Church**   30
   Prof. Frances Young

4 **Victorian Family Values**   47
   Dr Alistair Mason

5 **The Family, Religion and Feminism**   63
   Dr Grace Jantzen

6 **The Family in a Technological Society**   85
   Dr Jacqui Stewart

7 **The Abuse of Family**   103
   Dr Alistair McFadyen

8 **The Allure of Choice and the Force of Destiny**   119
   Prof. Gerard Rochford

9 **Family Life – School of Faith?**   131
   Prof. Haddon Willmer

PREFACE

The present collection of essays arises out of a series of lectures given under the auspices of the Department of Theology and Religious Studies of the University of Leeds from January to March 1995. The purpose of these lectures was to examine seriously the theological understanding of the family in the light of the variety of ways in which human beings live and love together. This variety means that even to define 'the family' is problematic; indeed, the issue of what is defined as a 'proper' family is one that is taken up repeatedly in the collection and the reader may not be helped by trying to pre-empt that discussion. The contributors themselves represent a wide spectrum of religious opinion and between them have experience of a great variety of family structures. What is common to all these essays is that they take seriously the role of the life and language of religious communities in shaping and reshaping the way in which humans nurture and are nurtured by each other as children, as partners, as lovers and as friends.

The topicality of the subject of religion and the family can hardly be doubted. Not a day goes by without a report or a newspaper headline involving 'the family'. In most cases, the family is portrayed as a beleaguered institution under attack as part of a wider breakdown of social institutions. The decline in the family is often linked to declining social morality, rising crime and the lack of respect and self respect in the young. Amongst those who see this decline, however, debate rages on its cause and how to counter it. Is the breakdown of traditional family structures to be seen as a symptom of social upheaval, mobility, unemployment and poverty or is it rather a cause of these? Attitudes differ widely and contentiously. In complete contrast, however, are those who see the decline of traditional structures as a movement of liberation and not any kind of disaster. A whole spectrum of oppressed groups – women and children, gays and lesbians among them – are, according to this argument, in the process of being freed from the tyranny of a social structure designed to shore up the power of men in a patriarchal society.

In such debates, religion is constantly invoked. Religious institutions and communities are seen as the guardians of the moral order. For those on the right, a failure of moral leadership is seen as a prime cause of the present situation. In a so-called Christian society, the churches have failed to stand up to the inroads of sexual immorality. For those on the left, the churches have failed by passively condoning the economic and social degradation of large sections of the population. They stand accused of failing to exercise a prophetic ministry to the political and financial leaders of society. For the most radical, religious institutions themselves represent the epitome of the patriarchal structure and are irredeemably tainted with its injustice.

As the established church, the Church of England has particularly borne the weight of these attacks. The recent report of the working party of the Board of Social Responsibility, chaired by the Bishop of Sherwood, which appeared just as this collection was going to press, is entitled *Something to Celebrate*. That such a title should be chosen indicates that its authors feel they have to dispel an atmosphere of gloom over the family. They set out to affirm the majority of people who are working hard to make a success of their relationships and to take responsibility for children and the elderly. They find cause to rejoice in the qualities of loving selflessness which surface in all sorts of human situations, even those which others might deem unsatisfactory. A particularly valuable aspect of the report is its concise but telling overview of the immense variety of situations in which people live in Britain today. This, together with a brief but illuminating account of the history of the family, sets the context of the debate admirably. Readers of the present collection are warmly recommended to look there for such information.

Something to Celebrate, however, is set firmly within that strand of Christian tradition which affirms the value of family and parenthood. There are other strands, however, which seem to set much less value on the family as an institution. St Paul in some of his writings certainly seems to prefer that people should refrain from marriage. The report has good pragmatic and pastoral reasons for choosing to uphold the basis of family life and reflects wisely on its modern dilemmas, but religion, and specifically the Christian religion, cannot simply be reduced to the pragmatic. The idea of 'the Christian family' is one that has grown and developed over the centuries and both history and theology may raise questions about the legitimacy and form of any such concept. These are exactly the sort of questions that the present volume hopes to raise. It does not offer a commentary on that report, but rather an attempt to offer a kaleidoscope of theological reflections on the family which are faithful attempts to think through issues over the whole nature of the family which are beyond that report's remit.

The collection begins with the contribution of Dr John Habgood, the former Archbishop of York. In it he offers a characteristically lucid and measured personal defence of the importance of the family group centred round a married couple and their children in the face of all the difficulties and criticisms levelled at it. The proper nurture of children is central to his argument for a stable and committed form of family life. The ideal of the Christian family which he puts forward is, he argues, something to be cherished to carry us through the very real problems which threaten to disrupt familiar social patterns. It is in and through the family that wider social values are transmitted insofar as it acts as a 'school of charity'. In the course of his argument, he points out the increasingly uncertain position of men in our society and questions the validity of the conscious choice of single parenthood. He also calls for a review of the laws of divorce to remove the requirement to prove fault. Overall, his contribution represents a powerful statement of the central values of the tradition of the Christian family.

The papers that follow take up many of the themes he identifies and sometimes represent a sharp challenge to the traditional view. In this context, an appeal is often made to biblical values as a defence of the familial structure. Frances Young and Hugh Pyper both seek to bring out the ambivalence of the biblical and early Christian traditions over the family. Hugh Pyper shows how the New Testament takes up a profoundly subversive strand of Old Testament thinking as it seeks to transfer to

the church the traditional loyalty to the family. The attempt
to invoke the Bible as the foundation of an ordered society fails
to recognise its potential for disruption and in the case of the
family, he argues, risks making an idol of a human institution.
Frances Young looks at the development of the twin vocations
of marriage and celibacy in the early church and traces the
influence of Graeco-Roman social custom on the developing
church. Much of what is seen as the Christian model of the
family, she argues, in fact more nearly reflects the Stoic values
of late antiquity. Just as the church then was inevitably influ-
enced by the prevailing social mores, so the question for the
modern church becomes one of responsible engagement with
the wider culture rather than the attempt to defend a particular
social model which is not specifically Christian.

One such model, invoked either as a lost ideal or a dreadful
warning, is the Victorian family and its values. In an intriguing
investigation based on the best-selling children's books of Mrs
Sherwood which appeared in many editions throughout the
nineteenth century, Alistair Mason shows how the ideal of the
family changed over this period, and how this was related to
theological developments in the understanding of God as
Father. A new emotional intensity forms the basis of the
relationships within families and this colours the use of family
metaphors in explanations of the relationship between Father
and Son in the Trinity and in the believer's relationship to
God. The Victorian family as such never existed, of course.
At best, this label represented a very particular and evolving
synthesis of social and religious values which cannot be encap-
sulated in a slogan or easily reproduced today, even should
we wish to. The late twentieth century offers a very different
world.

One of the major developments since the Victorian times
which has affected the contemporary family is the change in
the position of women. Grace Jantzen argues that families are
literally different places for women and men. Men think of
them in terms of security and relaxation, women in terms of
work and duty. The structures function to maintain the power
of men. She argues that there is no necessary opposition
between the religious view of the family and feminist models

once the equation between God, maleness and power is broken. The family life of Jesus himself puts this equation in question, she argues. This paper is a strong statement of the value of the freedom to choose our family structures and argues that this freedom is more characteristic of the Christian tradition than the narrow patriarchal models which are often identified with it. The reader will find much to ponder in the juxtaposition of this paper with Dr Habgood's.

On a related topic, Jacqui Stewart explores the topic of technology and the family. She examines the way in which changes in housing, domestic technology and communications have all had an impact on the family. In the name of technological advance, people have been induced or forced to adopt patterns of life which actually reduce their ability to devote time and energy to their children. Women, in particular, have, despite appearances, not been freed by modern housing and domestic appliances to restructure their family lives. She makes use of the insights of the French theologian Jacques Ellul as to the way in which the seemingly objective language of technology is used to disguise debates which are really about values. She reminds us of the particular duty of the theologian to call attention to these underlying values.

Something to Celebrate inevitably but unfortunately entered the tabloid headlines on the strength of one brief reference. It talks of the unhelpfulness of the concept of 'living in sin' to describe those who cohabit before marriage. Quite apparently, there are very few of us who do not live in sin in some aspect of our lives and the range and scope for sinfulness in married relationships is vast. If the use of this term blinds us to the sins of violence, abuse and neglect which can mar family life, then it is not only unhelpful but harmful. Al McFadyen's contribution on 'The Abuse of Family' is a sensitive search for a theological understanding of what is fundamentally *abusive* in the sorry catalogue of sexual and physical insults which family members may inflict on each other. He points to the real sin in these situations as the stunting of the capacity for trust and therefore of joy through the misappropriation of power. He also explores the tricky subjects of the meaning of consent and the place of will and choice in abusive relationships. His paper will be of interest to all those concerned with this dark side of family life in its attempt to give a broader theological perspective to the issues.

Underlying so many of these questions is a fundamental theological question about the freedom of human beings to choose who they are and how they are to live. As the use of birth control has increased, and medical technology has widened the range of choice such questions have become more complex. What were once presented as unchallengeable givens of human society are now open to question and revision. To marry or not to marry, to have children or not, to carry a handicapped child to term or not, to accept one's physical sex or to change it, these are all questions demanding choice for us now which either never confronted our ancestors or which had clear and socially determined answers. Such dilemmas of choice and acceptance are explored by Gerald Rochford. As choice seems to increase for adults and parents, we should not forget that there never can be a reciprocal freedom for children. We will never be able to choose who conceived us. The dilemma about how far we must accept what we are given and how far it is our duty or right to strive to change it is at the heart of our relationships with our parents, our society, our selves and our God.

The volume is completed with a contribution from Haddon Willmer who takes as his key theme the words of the angel to Mary when she is warned that a sword will pierce her heart. Families are about commitment and about the pain and joy which people inflict on those they love most dearly. In families, we are confronted with the inescapable realities of human life and the more or less adequate ways in which we try to cope with them. They are about vulnerability, limitation, trust, betrayal and forgiveness. Families are not there to guarantee happiness for their members, and the expectation that they will is the cause of much disappointment. Rather, they are real schools in the truth of human being, and as with any real school, they cannot offer a guarantee of an easy ride or a spectacular success to every one. That, however, is no reason to give up on the family. Part of what we most need to learn is the resourcefulness to cope with the less than perfect in the struggle to win faith and to win our own and our collective humanity.

Families matter to people, and so does religion. Everyone who has reached the stage of being able to think about who they are and what they should do, must have been born to someone and must have been fed, nurtured, taught to walk and speak by someone. Some human community, however it was constructed, for good or ill, gave each of us our first training in human relations and set in place the patterns of response which we have carried forward in our own attempts to form adult relationships and to find our place in the continually self-renewing stream of human society. We may accept or reject what was done to us, but in either case, the importance of those first personal and social relationships is fundamental.

It is also in these first relationships that the questions of origins and destiny, of choice and acceptance which religion claims to address first confront us. The family will be our first school of religion. It may convey to us its own faith or lack of it, or else it may provoke in us a deep rebellion against all it stands for. For good or ill, however, the family and metaphors of the family are bound up with our experience of faith.

This gives to any discussion of the family a passion and an emotional investment which cannot be ignored. To attack the family is, in the eyes of its champions, to attack the basis of human social, moral and spiritual development. The attack not only damages the roots of our communal life, but the very foundation of its defenders' identity. But, for others, to defend the family is to defend an institution which they have found profoundly damaging, one which, they feel, has conspired to prevent them and others like them from developing as they should. The battle between the two rages over the heads of the great majority of people who are doing their best in an unstable world to bring some order and love into their own lives and the lives of young and old for whom they feel responsible. It is our hope that the discussions in this volume may make a contribution to the long process of public debate which will keep the importance of that central effort to the fore and affirm its profound religious significance.

1

THE FAMILY AND THE NEW SOCIAL ORDER[1]

John Habgood

I begin nearly twenty years ago when I visited a Kibbutz on the shore of the Sea of Galilee. It was impressive to encounter a community in which family distinctions had almost been abolished. Though married couples lived together, their children for the most part lived communally and only stayed with their parents for limited periods during the day. They were looked after by people who had been specially trained for the job, they appeared happy and well adjusted, and there was obviously a high degree of socialisation. There were interesting signs, though, even among what was still a first or second generation of kibbutz dwellers, that the pattern was not totally satisfying. Parents were increasingly concerned to have their children sleeping with them at night, and one sensed that before very long the parents' sleeping huts would come to be regarded as home.

The psychologist Bruno Bettelheim, writing about the kibbutz experience at about the same time in his book *The Children of the Dream*[2], noted similar signs. He described how the inspiration for kibbutz living came out of the experience of Jews in Central and Eastern Europe, frequently confined to ghettos, oppressed by tight-knit family structures, and wanting to escape into a new social order in which the demands of child rearing and the dominance of parents would no longer overshadow their lives. It was the pursuit of an ideal in which an open community life could break down barriers, and create a new sense of belonging.

But it had its costs. What Bettelheim particularly observed was the loss of individuality and intimacy. If everything is public, communal, well ordered and rationally planned, then

1

the times and places when one can simply be oneself disappear
or become constrained. Being oneself is what we do at home.
But if 'home' is a hut visited by children from 5.00 p.m. to
7.00 p.m., then it does not provide the kind of emotional
security children need. Parental care is controlled by the hands
of the clock. Security lies in the kibbutz as a whole, not in a
set of intimate relationships; and this makes it extremely hard
for individuals to stand out over against the community, or to
have ideas of their own.

I have started with this experience because it is the major
example of social engineering as applied to family life in the
last fifty years. It seems to illustrate how different patterns of
family life tend to produce different kinds of people. Discussions about the family, therefore, have much wider implications than the family itself. They are about the sort of society
we are creating for ourselves. To the extent to which this is
true, our contemporary concern in Britain about the family is,
or should be, central to social policy. The kibbutz experience
also illustrates the tension between communitarian ideals and
individualism; it reveals that behind differences of opinion
about different patterns of family life, there may lie deeper
ideological issues.

The family in today's Britain

In the new social order which has been emerging in Britain
(and much of the Western world) over the past quarter century
or so, we have been witnessing what some interpret as the de-
construction of the family. The statistics are all too familiar. One
divorce for every two marriages. Thirty-two per cent of all
births are outside marriage. Nineteen per cent of families with
dependent children have lone parents. One hundred and twenty
thousand abortions a year among unmarried women. Cohabitation on the increase, whether as a prelude to marriage or as an
alternative to it. We all know such figures, and they generate
a sense of crisis, particularly when linked in people's minds with
the crime statistics, the overwhelming proportion of which
relate to young men between the ages of fifteen to twenty-five.
Something seems to have gone wrong with the process of

socialisation, more so in men than in women, perhaps because men are more in need of the maturing effect of family responsibility. Thus growing uncertainties abut the viability of traditional patterns of family life are seen by some as a causal factor in some of the most obvious ills in our present society.

Others take a more sanguine view. Marriage is still enormously popular. Most people get married eventually, and the fact that an increasing proportion do it several times is an ironic reminder of its continuing importance, even to those who have experienced repeated failures. Furthermore, though the social conditions under which marriages exist may change, the bonding between husband and wife and the sense of responsibility for children are as old as humanity itself. They tend to reassert themselves even when, as in the kibbutzim, social engineering presses strongly in the opposite direction. The myth that the nuclear family is a recent phenomenon which underlies many of the present strains in family life is firmly discounted by those who see it as just one more way in which this fundamental bonding adapts itself to a more fragmented society. Indeed, it is hard to read the Bible and not to see there, in a very different cultural milieu, things which we can immediately recognise as belonging to our own experience of family life. The description in some of the Pauline epistles of the relationship between husband and wife implies an intimacy which belies the notion that romantic love was a much later invention.

But some things *have* changed, in particular three developments: the emancipation of women; the growing economic independence of the sexes; and the cultural and ideological changes which have given increasing importance to personal self-fulfilment. The conjunction of these three factors has meant that the crisis in marriage today is, as I have already indicated, to some extent a crisis abut the role of men. With changing patterns of employment, the diminution in what has traditionally been 'men's work', the apparently limitless opportunities for sexual encounters without responsibility, there is a growing body of men who feel that they have no particular stake in society, and who by and large are regarded by women as not worth marrying. It is this group of young men who now form the most visible manifestation of a society under strain and who, at least in part, are the victims of social changes outside their control. Their plight is made worse by their having to exist on the fringes of a culture which judges success in terms of self-gratification. I mention them at this stage because they are, as it were, the fall-out from processes of change which some see as having fatally and irreversibly weakened family life, but which others, including myself, believe can be surmounted.

The care of children

If it is true, as I suggested earlier, that different patterns of family life tend to produce different kinds of people, then the right starting-point for assessing the value of different patterns must be the basic needs of children, if they are to grow up capable of living responsible and fulfilled lives in society.

The children of the kibbutz enjoyed the security all children need, but they had little exposure to intimate relationships. Their emotional lives were mainly focused on the group. This may seem at first sight like a return to the much-praised concept of the extended family. But there is a subtle difference. An extended family has a structure, a hierarchy. Its members are bound together in organic relationships which themselves constitute a kind of intimacy, even though it may not be a strongly emotional one. In fact there are grounds for seeing the development of more strongly emotional attachments as one of the consequences of declining infant mortality. This is not to suppose that parents in earlier ages did not love their children – clearly many of them did. But with high infant mortality they had to safeguard themselves against investing too much of themselves in children, most of whom were likely to die young.

When greater personal involvement in the lives of children became less likely to have traumatic consequences, the family could become more close-knit, more geared to the needs of individuals, though in some instances more oppressive. The sturdy entrepreneurial individualism of the years from the mid-nineteenth century onwards owes something to this shift, as did the claustrophobic closeness against which the ghetto Jews reacted.

In our own day the death of a child is regarded as the ultimate tragedy – and understandably so. When one reads about the huge newspaper campaigns and money-raising efforts to send some hopelessly sick child to America or Russia for treatment, one realises how far the pendulum has swung. Indeed, might it perhaps in some cases have swung too far: can one always be sure that the efforts are being undertaken for the child's sake, rather than the parents'?

There is a proper balance between the deep attachment to individuals, and the acceptance that individuals need to exist in a multiplicity of relationships. No other person is ever wholly ours, not even our child. We need community as well as intimacy, intimacy as well as community. And when in adults we look for strength of character and sensitive awareness of others, a right blend of freedom and responsibility, it is in the balance between intimacy and community in childhood that we may hope to find its origins.

But if it is difficult to get this right with young children, it becomes much harder as they grow up. I suspect most of us are conscious of widespread bewilderment among parents about how to do their best for their children – and I am thinking here of conscientious parents, not those who have given up the struggle already. One factor in this bewilderment is the extent to which parents may feel de-skilled by the professional services available to their children from an early age. The family somehow seems less important than when most of the life-skills acquired by children had to be learnt within it. Furthermore, in a rapidly changing society the children may grow up in a world largely unfamiliar to their parents, under the influence of a powerful and class-transcending youth culture, reinforced by the media. There is thus a rapid loss of parental authority, and an increasing dependence on residual emotional attachments which may have become stuck at a particular stage of development. When parents complain that they have no control over their children, it may not be the result of weakness or fecklessness, but simply the end product of a long process of growing away from each other in an increasingly differentiated kind of society.

In describing this scenario I have in mind basically good and fairly traditional families, the families one would expect to be strong formers of character. If it is difficult in these, it must be immensely more difficult in families with deep internal divisions, the families of serial marriages, and families which lack stability, mutuality and trust. There are unresolved arguments abut the long-term consequences of divorce on the lives of the children involved. Scientifically it may be difficult to establish precise connections between the behaviour of parents and the emotional problems of their children. But I doubt whether most teachers need convincing that there *is* a connection. And while some children may become more self-reliant in the long term as a result of troubles at home, it is equally plain that others may suffer directly or indirectly for much of their lives.

The need for stability

I shall return to the question of divorce later, and to other patterns of family life as they have developed in recent decades. But still concentrating on what promotes the balanced development of children, I want to say a word about privacy. There is a nice architectural illustration of changing ideas about privacy in the historical growth of the archbishop's palace in York. It began in the thirteenth century as a Great Hall and a Chapel. That was all. Everything except worship happened in the Great Hall or in the basement beneath it. Life was totally public. They ate, worked, slept and prayed together. By the fourteenth century ideas were beginning to change, and two small rooms were built on the end of the hall for the use of the Archbishop. In the late fifteenth century this accommodation was enormously expanded, and it seems likely that members of the household, except servants, had their own bedrooms. But the house itself still retained a very open character, with no division between work areas and domestic areas until the mid-twentieth century. Nowadays even Archbishops demand some privacy, but it was only about twenty-five years ago that a private entrance was built for the Archbishop and his family.

Like the children of the kibbutz, all of us need a place where we can be ourselves and this has become more important as the pace and the demands of life have increased, and there are dangers for those whose public lives are constantly open to public scrutiny. I am not just thinking of shocking goings on, but of the need I referred to earlier for a home where it is possible for a certain inwardness to be developed, a deeper sense of individuality.

There are strong overtones in what I am saying of the need for prayer and silence, for pausing in life as the remedy against simply being entrapped in other people's demands and expectations. Translating this into family terms it seems to me that all of us, and perhaps particularly young people, need the kind of living space in which there is somewhere which is specially our own. The fact that this is impracticable for all too many families is maybe a further reason why the development of a strong responsible individuality is fraught with such difficulties.

There are plenty of ways in which the socialisation process I have been describing can go wrong. Emotional attachment can easily become oppressive and self-regarding. Intimacy can become exploitation and may be but a short step from abuse. Privacy can cloak selfishness, and seem to justify possessiveness. We may have seen the fruits of some of these in the kind of individualism which lacks moral direction as is seen solely as a means of personal fulfilment. A family life which is exclusively about emotional attachment, intimacy and privacy, lacks the very qualities of openness which gave the individualism of the nineteenth and early twentieth centuries its strength. It lacks the sense of being part of a larger whole and sharing a moral purpose. No wonder the kibbutz alternative looks attractive, and one can see its counterpart in other societies in the reaction against 'family values' – 'tawdry secrets' as they were once memorably described – and through experiments in communal living, and involvement in movements of various kinds from veal protesters to house churches.

But community values are also, or can be, fostered within families themselves. People sometimes speak as if the relational aspects of marriage can be entirely separated from the pro-creation and nurturing of children. Contraceptively, of course, they can, but psychologically it is not so easy. A *pas de deux* which systematically avoids the possibility of children runs the risk of self-absorption. I underline the word 'systematically'. Couples who desperately want children and are denied them can sometimes marvellously turn this longing into generosity towards others. But a fear of children who might place a strain on a 'good relationship', so called, is more likely to be a sign of immaturity.

If children can help a parental relationship to mature, then equally the quality of that relationship can be of vital importance to children. I like the description of family life as a 'school of charity'. A family is a tiny differentiated society, each member of which has a distinct role and individuality. If it can actually do its work as a school of charity, the chances are that it will lay the foundations for an individual's sense of stable identity in a meaningful society, an increasingly rare commodity in the world for which its members are being prepared.

When in the past I have expressed doubts about one-parent families, this is the concern which underlies them. I know that most one-parent families are not so by choice, and it is clear that many single parents do an excellent job in bringing up their children and should be given every possible support in doing so. A deliberate choice of single parenthood, however, seems to me to convey a very different message. It is about an unwillingness to enter into a mature reciprocal relationship and it must therefore fail to provide that schooling in charity, especially the charity between the sexes, which helps to balance intimacy and community.

The social meaning of marriage

The role of families within the larger society is another aspect of this community dimension in family life. I acknowledge that cohabitation is an increasingly popular alternative to marriage. But most Christians, I suspect, find it hard to countenance cohabitation as an alternative to marriage, despite the fact that our present marriage regulations are not yet two hundred and fifty years old. The commonly held claim that marriage is 'only a bit of paper' misses the central point. Though the registration of marriages is comparatively recent, and though forms of marriage may have changed, marriage itself has for many centuries been regarded as a fundamental social institution, and as such it has been able to carry meanings which transcend the couple concerned.

To reduce the family to a temporary liaison, or to think of marriage merely as a contract which can be broken as easily as it is made, is to empty it of much of its social meaning and fatally to weaken it as a social support for love and fidelity. It is also to ignore the reality of the new organic relationships to which the bearing of children necessarily gives rise. Children are not contractually related to their parents; they organically belong to them and they need to be able to trust that organic relationship as a constituent part of their own identity. The enduring social meaning of marriage ought to be able to provide a publicly recognised framework for that trust, independent of the particular state of personal relationships.

You will notice that, despite the obvious difficulties, I have been moving towards a very traditional view of marriage and family life. I have done so on the grounds that this is what children need, because it seems to me that it is as the optimum setting within which the emotional and developmental needs of children can be met, that the value of the traditional family is to be found. And I believe it is important that Christians at least, and I hope others alongside them, will not be deflected from this central insight. I have stressed the traditional family also because this is the direction in which a Christian understanding of marriage inescapably points. It is true that the Old Testament is not as strong on monogamy as it might have been, but it is quite clear on the subject of fidelity. It is also true that Jesus said some dismissive things about his own family. 'Who is my mother? Who are my brethren and sisters? . . . whosoever shall do the will of God, the same is my brother and sister and mother.' Families are not the be-all and end-all of existence. Families may misunderstand and frustrate us. No one can be a prophet in his own country. Conversely, there are dangers in any family that love and generosity may be concentrated entirely within the family itself in a form of higher selfishness, rather than extending to those outside.

Such a religious critique of family life has nothing in common, however, with contemporary efforts to deconstruct the family. The fact that obedience to God may override family loyalties and spell trouble at home does not devalue all that is associated with home and family. It merely puts it in a large context. For Jesus, home and family had to be transcended, just as early in the life of the Church Judaism, rooted as it was in the idea of descent, had to be transcended in what was to become a universal faith. But as we see in the Epistles, this is not the whole story. Marriage is a covenant relationship; it is about the God-given possibilities of love and faithfulness which are seen, both in the Old Testament and in the New, as in some way mirroring the relationship of love and faithfulness between God and his people. The Gospel message of families is that the love and faithfulness, and indeed the forgiveness, on which they depend, are not ours alone, but God's. The Epistle to the Ephesians which develops the analogy between man and wife, and Christ and the Church, is the high point of this interpretation of marriage as profoundly rooted in the idea of God's initiative in covenanting with us. And this in turn is what for Christians gives stability and purpose to life, both the attitude of Jesus towards family life, therefore, and the theology developed around family relationships elsewhere in the Bible, point beyond themselves to the God who encompasses and transcends and gives meaning to these relationships, together with the grace to sustain them.

I have taken you on this brief theological tour because my argument so far has been based on the needs of children, and on the need for certain qualities of character if people are to live freely, responsibly and creatively together. When one asks, why should couples without children, or with no possibility of having children, take marriage seriously, the argument becomes more difficult. I have sketched a theological answer. As human beings we need, and must practise, love and fidelity because that is how God expresses himself towards us, and that is therefore how we shall find our deepest fulfilment. I have also hinted earlier that creating a small school of charity is not only important for children but good for adults too. Neither of these answers may carry much conviction, though, with those who see human relationships as essentially transitory, and who look for short-term gratification rather than for enduring love. They may discover that, whatever the attractions of transitoriness, there is a heavy price to pay. Nevertheless, having said that, if changing social expectations make the prospect of permanent faithfulness seem less and less plausible, transitory happiness may not seem such a bad option.

There is, however, a further non-theological argument in favour of traditional marriage, even for the childless, which takes us back to what I said earlier about marriage as a social institution, rather than just a personal contract. The point about social institutions is that they provide a context to enable us to understand and shape our experience without having to start from scratch. We 'enter into marriage' as a state of life already thoroughly explored by others. Within that state of life we have to create our own marriage; and our chances of creating something worthwhile are, at least in theory, greatly enhanced because we are not simply dependent on our own resources. This is why lovers read love poetry and buy roses. But I add 'at least in theory' because norms and expectations and institutions can be destructive as well as creative. Unrealistic expectations and bad role models can frustrate good intentions. An over-romanticised view of marriage can make actual marriage difficult. Soap operas in which marital quarrels and infidelity are a main source of dramatic interest subtly change perceptions of what should be regarded as normal. The same is true within each marriage if individuals behave in ways which cumulatively weaken or strengthen the institutional supports of family life. This is why the quality of a particular marriage is not just the concern of that particular family. Insofar as we all depend on institutional norms, we also contribute to them and if we undermine them, we may be decreasing the life-possibilities of others.

Recently, I aroused considerable media interest by an off-the cuff remark about fiscal incentives to marriage. Changes in the tax system in recent years have gradually eroded distinctions between married couples and two individuals living together, and in some instances married couples actually fare worse in terms of tax than cohabitees.

Predictably, many people interpreted my remarks as a bid to attract more marriages back to the churches; there were angry responses from the single, the divorced and those whom I suspect would describe themselves as 'liberated'; and there were a surprisingly large number of morally superior comments from those whose love was untainted by money. But all these missed the main point, which was simply that if marriage is a socially important institution, then there need to be some socially significant distinctions between the married and those who adopt alternative forms of relationship. This is not bribery. It entails the recognition that some things go wrong in a way that runs *with* the grain of society, whereas other things go wrong in opposition to it, and that if we want to encourage certain forms of behaviour then we need to make sure that the grain of our society goes in that direction. To use the jargon, it is about social markers.

I feel the same about the current use of the word 'partner'. I know it is intended as a neutral and unembarrassing way of acknowledging different types of relationship. But what it also does is to prescribe a new norm. It is saying in effect that there is nothing particularly distinctive about being a husband or a wife. Is that what we want to say? It not only hides the truth of relationships, but it also provides a further impetus to think in purely contractual terms. Partnerships can dissolve at the drop of a hat. Marriages can't.

Divorce

I come therefore finally to the issue of divorce. Much of what I have been saying so far may have seemed impossibly idealistic and abstract. The reality of many marriages is not at all as I have described it. It is all very well to defend a traditional view of marriage and the family, say the realists, but these were never as ideal as they were supposed to be, and now in a more open society our forms of relationship can be less hypocritical.

I grant that realism is essential, but not surely a realism which has lost hold of ideals and has no vision of what it wants to strive for. Nor is what I have been saying *mere* idealism, because plenty of people achieve something like it and I have argued that it is vital for the future health of our society. But there has to be room also for failure, and that is why I have also argued in recent years for better divorce laws and a more understanding approach by the Church of England towards those whose marriages are broken.

In particular, I have strongly supported the latest attempts by the Lord Chancellor to define a more satisfactory basis for recognising marriage breakdown without using the concept of fault. This is not to claim that fault plays no part in the reasons why marriages break down. Frequently all too many people are at fault. The point is, though, that if fault is made the basis of the divorce then the whole issue becomes confrontational as soon as divorce proceedings are initiated. This entails increased trauma for the couple and their children, a probable legacy of bitterness, and a denial of the possibility of reconciliation before the full implications of divorce have been explored. By contrast, there is a human dignity which can be preserved, even in the face of failure and, without going into further details, I believe the Lord Chancellor's proposals can help to achieve this. I believe more civilised divorce procedures, not necessarily easier ones but less confrontational, could help married couples feel that the law is on their side in helping them to face up to the full implications of what they are doing and in enabling them to work through their problems. And I believe that better procedures could, paradoxically, strengthen marriage itself and perhaps in some cases save it.

Conclusion

Family life in our new social order is clearly under strain. We can accept the new patterns which are emerging, with all their unknown consequences. Or we can seek to strengthen and support family life as it has developed in our culture so that it provides a stable, humanly attractive and, I believe, much needed foundation for the formation of future generations. The choice is ours.

NOTES

1. This paper represents the author's personal reflections on the wider topic of religion and the family. It was written, and delivered as a lecture, sometime before the publication of the report by a Church of England working party *Something to Celebrate* and is not therefore a response to it.

2. London, Thames and Hudson; 1969.

2

THE FAMILY IN THE BIBLE

Hugh Pyper

In his much-loved poem 'The Cotter's Saturday Night', Burns writes of the poor but upright family which to him reveals the essence and backbone of the simple, honest peasant folk who were the glory of Scotland.

> The chearfu' supper done, wi' serious face
> They, round the ingle, form a circle wide;
> The sire turns o'er, wi' patriarchal grace,
> The big *ha'-bible*, ance his Father's pride.[1]

The little family clusters reverently round to hear 'the priest-like Father read ... the sacred page'.[2] The vignette that Burns chooses to reveal the unity of his family is the gathering centred on reading of the biblical text. 'From scenes like these', as Burns famously, or notoriously, asserts, 'old Scotia's grandeur springs'. It is from this archetypal moment, Burns implies, that the well-ordered world of the cotter is sustained. His own humble but honest toil, the canny housewifery of his beloved spouse, the obedience and respect for duty instilled in the children are rooted in the decent reading of the family Bible.

Nor should we overlook the fact that this Bible represents not just the focus of the family, but quite explicitly represents its continuity. This was his father's book, handed down to him and, more than likely, the history of the family itself is inscribed in its pages. In careful copperplate, births, marriages and deaths within this little lineage are listed on the end papers of this book. It becomes a record of memory, a testament to genealogy. This family in its humble way is aligned with the great genealogies of the text, the line that runs from Adam to Abraham, from Abraham to David, and from David to Christ – or at least to Joseph.

The poem also contains a somewhat arch glance towards the

future of the family. The chaste but ardent passion of young Jenny who has been brought home by a young man is legitimated by the bashfulness and gravity of her swain. His reverent carriage proves him to be of a different metal, so Burns avers, from the smooth dissembler who would ruin the maid and leave her parents distracted. The decent ordering of sexual relations that will ensure in generations to come the existence of a family worthy to receive in their turn the gift of the great Bible is thus assured. It is, Burns asserts, such families and such lives which will be as a 'wall of fire' around the nation.

The dark side of the biblical family

What a comforting picture, what a model of stability to set forth to a modern world of marriage breakdown, divorce, child abuse, teenage anomie and sexual libertarianism – although the latter at least was perhaps more characteristic of the poet himself than this domestic idyll. And yet, one cannot help wondering what passages of the Bible were being read. For instance, was it, one wonders, the story of Lot's daughters seducing their father by getting him drunk (Gen. 19.30–38)? Or what about the story of the bold Tamar, praised in Genesis 38, who became ancestress to David by posing as a prostitute and seducing her father-in-law? How would the communal reading of such scandalous exploits accord with the world of the respectable family in the poem?

Perhaps it might be argued that such shenanigans are all that can be expected of the Old Testament – although Tamar makes her appearance in Matthew's version of Jesus' genealogy.[3] Let us turn then to the New Testament. Can we suppose that this pious father was reading Jesus' words as reported by Luke: 'If anyone comes to me and does not hate his own father and mother and wife and children and brothers and sisters . . . he cannot be my disciple' (Luke 14.26)? Somehow one doubts it. But this brings us to the question we must ask: what model of family is being presented in such a teaching?

Of course, it could be said that to select such passages is a distortion, made simply to provide an easy point. The biblical tradition is, everyone knows, family based. From Adam and

Eve, through the great rehearsals of genealogy, the stories of
families form the bulk of its histories. 'Honour thy father and
mother', says the fourth of the ten commandments,[4] cited
approvingly by the writer of the letter to the Ephesians in the
New Testament.[5] What clearer endorsement of the family could
we look for than that? The biblical story begins with the creation of the human male/female couple, enjoined to be fruitful,
and the recognition of Eve by Adam as his 'apt companion' is
crowned by the aetiological note, 'therefore a man leaves his
father and his mother and cleaves to his wife, and they become
one flesh' (Gen. 2.24). The family is established as a presuppo-
sition to the story. Yet here already there is a potential ambivalence: 'honour your father and mother' – and leave them. The
new family can only be formed by the breaking of the old. And
notice that there is nothing said on the bond between parent
and child in these texts. The first chapters of Genesis are no
substitute for the likes of Dr Spock on child-rearing. Our
modern and legitimate concern for the well-being of a child
and the reciprocal affection of parents and children is not the
focus of attention.

If we look a little deeper, indeed, we discover that far from
being celebrated by the text, the begetting and raising of children is presented to us more as a contingency plan, at times
almost a necessary evil. In the face of death, which, once the
fruit of the tree is eaten, both man and woman have to confront
and deal with, the problem of survival becomes the text's key
concern. Life now becomes an unending battle to stave off
death. The family made up of man, woman and children is a
structure of survival.[6]

'Kin, Cult, Land and Afterlife'

The system of ideas which cluster around it in the Hebrew
Scriptures is well expressed in the title of a paper by Herman
Brichto: 'Kin, Cult, Land and Afterlife – A Biblical Complex.'[7]
He argues that the particular form of the family as an institution
in the Hebrew traditions is characterised by the way it mediates
all these aspects. So identity in the Hebrew Bible is established
by lists of male ancestors, male because it was through the

male seed that life was thought to be transmitted. Woman's contribution was to be the field in which the seed was planted; the necessary matrix for the continuation of life, but not its source.[8] Immortality, the afterlife, was also to be ensured by the future projection of this lineage, by supplying a line of legitimate male descendants who would 'remember one's name'. It is at least plausible that this concept of 'remembering the name' was for much of Israel's history linked to a cult of the ancestors where sacrifice and prayers were offered on behalf of ancestral spirits.[9]

Be that as it may, the link between the legitimate lineage and the prospect of survival or remembrance beyond death is clear. Yet this has profound consequences for the ordering of social relations. For men to ensure that their sons are their own descendants, they must put unassailable boundaries around the sexual activity of women. As the Latin legal tag has it; *mater certus est, pater incertissimus*: the mother is certain, the father is extremely uncertain. Only by draconian regulations can men allay the ever-present suspicion that their wives' children are not their own.

In this context of the necessity of maintaining the family line, it is thus possible to comprehend seemingly bizarre provisions such as the so-called levirate, the legislation for which is outlined in Deuteronomy 25.5–10. This was the custom whereby a childless widow was entitled to expect to be married to her dead husband's brother in order to raise children who would keep up the remembrance of the dead man's name and maintain his legal claims to inheritance. The overriding nature of the need to secure survival is made apparent.[10]

The topics of the relationship of such a model of social order to the development of patriarchy on the one hand and the growth of the concepts of private property and inheritance are intriguing and highly relevant but beyond the scope of this essay.[11] For our purpose, the important thing to note is that such a system carries within it inevitable tensions. For women, it means that they have to surrender control of their sexuality to men. For men, it means that their hope of immortality and continuity depends on the fidelity of women. For fathers, it means that a son is both necessary for their survival, but also a constant reminder of death and a constant possible rival for the ownership and governance of the household. For a son, it means that his life and prospects depend on his father's largesse until his death. As a younger son, his prospects are blocked by both his father and his elder brothers. Ancient Israelite society, like many other societies ancient and modern, knew the necessity of finding ways of dealing with superfluous young men (in Biblical Hebrew the *ne'arim*) who drank, wenched and warred with no sense of economic responsibility because they were excluded from the property base and from the prospects of marriage within their society. We need not look far for modern parallels, as Dr Habgood reminds us in his paper.

So the story of the family is bound to be one of ambivalences, of jealousies, rivalries and deaths. Cain kills his brother Abel and things proceed from there. The family becomes the arena of the breakdown of human relations precisely because it is the centre of expectations of nurture, of fulfilment, of life itself. At the core of this ambivalence is that fact that the family is designed to ensure survival not of the individual but of the line, the 'name'. It may then well happen that the family will sacrifice one of its members to the common good, or that individuals will come to feel that their own prospects of survival would be increased by the removal of rivals or the disruption of the family. The inherent instability of the family over time as one generation gives place to another also means that power inevitably shifts, alliances have to be reforged, claims have to be settled. Such negotiations are fraught with the possibility of failure.

Against the family

So it is not surprising, whatever our initial expectations, to find that the Hebrew Scriptures are not only filled with tales of family conflict but that they also contain a series of counter-traditions which seek to repudiate the family, traditions in which the claims of father over son and son over father are denied or reformulated. A striking example is to be found in Ezekiel 20, one of the oddest chapters in a very puzzling book. It contains a startling reversal of the injunction to honour one's parents. God says to his people, 'Do *not* walk in the statues of your fathers; do not follow your fathers' abominations' (Ezek. 20.18). Even more shockingly, Ezekiel has God say, 'I gave them statutes that were not good and ordinances by which they could not have life' (Ezek. 20.25).

This is a far cry from honouring one's parents and their traditions. This is permission to the new generation to make a new start, to forge their own traditions. Such a note of rebellion shows how near at times the Hebrew Scriptures get to advocating the overthrow of the reign of the father. The rebellion stops short, however, of open hostility.

On the other hand, the biblical reticence does not extend to the reciprocal aspect of the assault on the mutual responsibilities of the family: the possibility of filicide, of a father killing his child. That most disturbing yet influential of biblical stories, the binding of Isaac in Genesis 22, gains much of its awesome power from its exploration of the turning of a parent against a child, both in the story of the expulsion of Ishmael and the story of the sacrifice of Isaac.

The passage in Ezekiel to which we have already referred to continues with a chilling hint of something akin to this. After the Lord's amazing admission that he had given bad laws to Israel's fathers, he goes on to say, 'I have defiled them through these very gifts by making them offer by fire all their first born, that I might horrify them; I did it that they might know that I am the Lord (Ezek. 20.26)'.

Debate has long raged over the existence of child sacrifice and the nature of the so-called cult of Molekh in Israel.[12] More often than not, the discussion seems to be animated by a concern to show that this practice could not have existed, rather than to investigate whether or not it did. There certainly is biblical and extra-biblical evidence to suggest that child sacrifice did occur, in the face of the obvious disapproval of the later editors of the biblical text who see this as the epitome of the corruption of the cults of Israel's neighbours. Whatever the truth of the matter, this passage in Ezekiel plainly claims not only that such a practice existed, but that it existed by Yahweh's decree. Shocking as this may seem, it is not the only instance of a definite strand in the biblical traditions where parents turn against their children in contexts which are sanctioned rather than condemned by the text. It surfaces, for instance, in Zechariah where the parents of a child who prophesies are enjoined to pierce him through.[13]

Most blatant, though, is the reference in Deuteronomy 21.18–21. In this passage, provision is made for the parents of a 'stubborn and rebellious son', one who will not mend his ways even after chastisement, to bring their errant offspring before the elders at the gate of the city and denounce him as a glutton and a drunkard. This denunciation in itself is sufficient to require the men of the city to stone the boy to death. The death of the son is necessary to purge this evil from the midst of Israel. What a disturbing picture of the seeming destruction of the family: a case where parents turn on their own children and blot out their own chance of survival, in the interests of the maintenance of the wider social conventions which are necessary to safeguard the survival of the people.

Not unnaturally, this passage seems to have caused considerable disquiet to later rabbinic commentators who exercised their ingenuity to bring it into harmony with their concern to affirm family solidarity. It is discussed at length in Tractate Sanhedrin of both the Mishnah and Talmud.[14] The conditions which must be fulfilled before such a sentence can be passed become increasingly stringent both as to the nature of the offence and the circumstances of the parents. Indeed, the Jerusalem Talmud ultimately concludes that the law as it stands is so difficult to apply and seemingly illogical that its purpose can only be to remind us that God's laws are not predicated on human reason, while R. Simeon declares roundly in the Babylonian Talmud, ' "A stubborn and rebellious son" – there never was and there never will be such.'[15] The passage exists only as an awful but ultimately unenforceable warning.

The rebellious son

Or does it? I want to argue that the disturbing figure of the disobedient son and his wrathful parents is one which echoes through the biblical traditions. The book of Hosea, for one, takes the highest analogy and speaks of a God who is quite prepared to bring his beloved son Israel before the tribunal of history and to threaten him with utter destruction for his disobedience.[16] This is not the God who is the shepherd of the much-loved Psalm 23, but a God who speaks of himself as a lion, a leopard, a she-bear without her cubs which will turn on the flock. God is revealed as the father who will, *in extremis*, do away with his stubborn and rebellious son.

And on the other side of the coin, what are we to make of a young man who, as we have already seen, says to his followers that unless they hate their father and mother thy cannot follow him (Luke 14.26),[17] who proclaims that he has come to set father against son, son against father, mother against daughter and so on (Luke 12.53), and who repudiates his own relatives including his mother when they come to fetch him home with the words 'Who are my mother and brothers?', answering himself 'Whoever does the will of God is my brother and sister and mother' (Mark 3.31–35)?[18] What could be a clearer case of the dishonouring of father and mother and of wilful disobedience?[19] In such statements, Jesus, the unmarried, rootless teacher, is spokesman for a new world, one where the human ties of family are not the means to ensure survival but an obstacle to living the abundant life. What is promised in the gospels is no mere continuity of the human comedy, but the utterly radical breaking down of the structures of human society and human personhood. His teaching in the New Testament is not predicated on survival but on resurrection which must call into question the nature of the family as a device for survival.

Clearly, then, it is no accident that when the Sadducees seek to entrap Jesus on the issue of resurrection, they cite the legislation on levirate marriage, that bizarre device to ensure survival.[20] This encounter shows starkly the incompatibility of the two world views of survival and resurrection. The Sadducees ask Jesus to explain to whom a woman would be deemed to be married in the resurrection if she had been given as wife to seven brothers in succession. Matthew and Mark both record Jesus as explaining that no one marries or is given in marriage in the resurrection as they are like angels in heaven. Once the threat of death has been overcome, the need for procreation is at an end and the elaborate devices of the levirate become irrelevant. Luke, however, goes further in drawing a distinction not between the living and those in the resurrection but between the 'sons of this age' who marry and the unmarried state of those who are 'accounted worthy to attain to that age and the resurrection of the dead' (Luke 20.34–35). This at least suggests that the unmarried state is a mark in this life of those who are destined for resurrection, not simply a consequence of the resurrected state.

This startling dismissal of marriage and the countervailing esteem given to the unmarried state has no parallel in the Hebrew Scriptures and is completely at odds with the positive duty to marriage that the rabbinic tradition enjoins.[21] In this regard, Jesus would seem by his own celibacy to be setting at naught the requirement for the line to continue. The genealogies which introduce him in Matthew and Luke's gospels are parodic subversions of the genealogical form. They never actually reach Jesus in whom the whole concept of the family line is brought to a close.

Even where, exceptionally, Jesus' teaching appears to buttress the institution of the family, other readings are possible. His repudiation of the Mosaic provision of divorce, by which he may seem to shore up the ideal of the family, has been seen by Jewish commentators as an attack on the continuity of the wider family, not a defence of it.[22] It binds partners to sterile or incompatible unions which lead to an involution and destruction of the continuity of the lineage. There is in Jesus's ruling on divorce what we might call an Edenic impracticality. The passage explicitly recalls the notion of man and woman becoming one flesh in Genesis. Marriage here becomes an expression of the ontological union of human partners, a metaphor for the union of Christ and his church according to Paul, rather than a pragmatic accommodation to the imperatives of child-rearing.

The chosen family

Family, then, is reinterpreted as a matter of choice, not heredity. In the gospel view, all the elements that Brichto saw as clustered round the concept of the family – kin, cult, land and afterlife – are subsumed in the radical action of God in resurrection. Jesus' call is to a resurrection which renders irrelevant all the human institutions designed to ensure survival. Such a call threatens profoundly all those whose understandable concern is to survive and to safeguard the continuance of their families and their culture.

It may not be a common move to draw a parallel in this regard between Jesus and the disobedient son of Deuteronomy, but it is there to be drawn. His fate, like that of the rebellious son, is to be put to death for his refusal to comply with the careful conventions of human society, so cunningly contrived to outwit the contingencies of death. Both threaten a radical unstructuring of human institution. Yet such a reading illumines the way in which the figure of Jesus in the gospel narratives acts as a focus for the tensions inherent in the biblical model of the family. Jesus, the obedient son of God, slain by his father for the disobedience of others, is also the one slain by the human wrath of those who see him as a blasphemous betrayer of the familial structure. He is one who flouts his own responsibilities, disrupts the family life of his followers and places at the centre of his teaching the abominable claim that he is God's son rather than that of his human father. But he is also identified by the tradition with the Father deserted and betrayed by those who had allied themselves to him as his spiritual children. In this tradition there is at once a convergence, a manifestation and a confrontation of the anxieties of anonymity, of abandonment, of the terror of forgetfulness which erupt through the stories of the biblical tradition. The filicidal tradition of the Hebrew Scriptures is both vindicated and transcended in this apotheosis where Jesus becomes the triumphant victim of a human patriarchy that cannot allow, because it cannot survive, his radicality.

This world where marriage and family are subordinated to the affiliative family of the church is also the one to be found in Paul's letters. The social and theological consequences of this are explored more fully in Frances Young's consideration of the family in the early church. At this point, we shall limit ourselves to continuing to pursue the theme of the relationship between parents and children beyond our exploration of the Hebrew tradition.

The fact is that it is hard to find any positive injunction to childbearing and child-rearing in the New Testament. It scarcely even appears as an issue until the later epistles. In 1 Timothy, child-rearing is recommended, but only as a means of placing a check on women's proclivity to sin. Women will be saved by childbirth and young widows, who otherwise will 'grow wanton against Christ', are to marry, bear children and to rule their households in order that the enemy may have no excuse to revile the church. These and other provisions mark the accommodation of the later New Testament writers to the inescapable fact that children are being born into the church, husbands are dying and life is continuing. It also marks the re-emergence of the need to control women's sexuality, a need which the radical teaching of Jesus makes irrelevant. Freed from the ties of property, family and sexuality, there is a glimpse of a new equivalence between men and women which soon succumbs to the realities of continued social existence.

The church then takes it upon itself the task of ensuring survival, but carries in its traditions a deep ambivalence about the role of family, tradition and property. Other papers in this volume explore the consequences of this, but the fundamental point that must be established here is this: these ambivalences over the dynamics of the family are not simply the product of some contemporary angst, some departure from biblical faithfulness, but are right at the heart of the biblical tradition itself. Nor does this reflect any simple polarisation of New Testament radicalism versus the conservatism of the Hebrew tradition. Both testaments know both tendencies.

Biblical values today

This encapsulates the problem in using the biblical tradition to come to grips with the changing role of the family in contemporary society. The biblical tradition offers no cure for the consequences of our ambivalence to the family. Rather, it offers a range of partially successful strategies of survival adopted, adapted and abandoned by the various communities who have sought to live out their existence under the consciousness of existence under the reign of God. Here, indeed, is the heart of the matter. The biblical tradition makes no coherent sense without this overarching unity conferred by the enigmatic figure of its God.

It is not the purpose of this paper to explore the interminable problems raised by such a claim. But without addressing this claim, there is no sense in looking to the biblical tradition as a source of guidance in human affairs. The writer to the Ephesians is to be taken entirely seriously when he says in Eph. 3.14–15 'For this reason I bow my knees before the Father, from whom every family on earth is named'. The biblical tradition of using the metaphors of family, of fatherhood and motherhood to express the relationship between God and the human sphere can only be taken on board if we are prepared to accept the notion that it is the human family, the human structure of relationships which is a metaphor for God's relationship to humankind, to Israel, to Jesus and to the church.

The biblical picture is of a structure of human relationships which obliquely and imperfectly reflects the relationship of God with his Son, whether that son is Israel or Jesus. In contemporary society, this model of the ordering of human relationships has now been evacuated of the disturbing presence of God. The family itself – that poor, abstract, ramshackle, ambivalent concept – then becomes the basis for the right ordering of personal, sexual and social relationships. From the point of view of the biblical tradition, this is nothing more or less than idolatry: an idolatry of the family. Who can wonder, then, that when the going gets tough and problems arise, we fall into the age-old patterns of behaviour of the idolaters so mercilessly derided in the book if Isaiah?[23] Staggering under the dead-weight of the idols we hoped would ensure our survival, in the panic of flight we end up throwing these unwieldy burdens into the ditch. The structures by which we seek to ensure our collective survival can themselves become the chains that shackle us to intolerable situations. If the biblical traditions are viewed merely as ethical prescriptions which act to shore up such failing human structures, then it is little wonder that they too are cast aside as burdens rather than seen as a summons to new life.

What the biblical tradition can do is to hold before us these tensions and irreconcilabilities. It does not attempt to provide an easy integration of them. The communities which use the Bible are thus in a position to maintain continuity through discontinuity by activating different, even antithetical, aspects of the tradition because the tradition itself has accumulated through just such a process of readings, rereadings and mis-readings. But this does entail the inevitability that the appeal to the biblical tradition to shore up our institutions brings with it not just the wood but the termites, to coin a phrase. We cannot appeal to one tradition as authoritative without having to accept other less amenable traditions as equally authoritative.

The radical critique of the family which is to be found in the gospels and Paul is not reducible to any liberal agenda of social reform or any conservative politics of social control. The Bible, to borrow the title of R.P. Carroll's recent book, is a 'wolf in the sheepfold'.[24] It is not a sheep dog. Those who do try to use it as such should realise the risk they run. It has taken centuries of domestication and cross-breeding to produce the structures of social morality whose collapse is now bewailed, structures which claim a dim ancestry in the biblical tradition but which have absorbed much of the ethos of the Greek and Roman traditions in the course of their evolution. When the wolf prowls, the sheep dogs bristle and howl, now the implac-able enemies of their wild ancestors. So, too, the radical elements of the biblical tradition are often most threatening to those who are most inclined to appeal to the Bible as bolstering their vision of the Christian family. The biblical tradition is a wild, undomestic, unfamiliar one for us.

What this tradition can do for us now is to call into question the idolatry of the family which is one truly destructive force in contemporary society. It can remind us that the virtues of fidelity and self-giving nurture which the family embodies at its best are not somehow definitively consigned to one structure of human relationships. Such values are not best assured by making an idol of a particular social structure. Conversely, placing the family in this wider context of relationships para-doxically may strengthen it as an institution by showing its limitations. The whole pressure of human aspiration, of human sin, does not have to be contained by this structure. It is not a failure of the family as such if it cracks under such a strain but of a society which has no sense of the transcendent which alone could bear that strain. The biblical tradition points to ways of living which are not dependent on the survival of this particular structure of survival. In this context, the family still, of course, has a role, but a contingent one. In this time of waiting, it provides the arena in which the virtues of patient communality can be practised.

NOTES

1. R. Burns *Poems and Songs* ed. James Kinsley (Oxford, OUP; 1971) p. 119, ll. 100–103

2. ibid. l. 118

3. See Matt. 1.3. She is one of four dubious women to appear in this genealogy, the others being Rahab, Ruth and the wife of Uriah, all of whom are associated with the defects of foreignness and extra-marital sexuality.

4. Ex. 20.12; Lev. 19.3; Deut. 5.16.

5. Eph. 6.2

6. This is almost explicit in the fourth commandment, which, as Eph. 6.2 reminds us, is the first commandment to be attached to a promise, a promise of long life and prosperity in the land or, in a word, of survival.

7. *Hebrew Union College Annual* 44 (1973): 1–54.

8. For a discussion of the models of reproduction in the ancient world and their effect on the position of women and the understanding of human nature generally, see Julia Stonehouse *Idols to Incubators: Reproduction Theory throughout the Ages* (London, Scarlet Press; 1994), in particular chapter 11: 'Portrait of a Takeover: Yahweh'.

9. The commandment to honour one's mother and father can be interpreted as a reference to just such a cult. The duty to honour one's parents is not confined to their lifetime, and maintenance of this cult is necessary for the prosperity and survival of the community. On this point, see E. Bloch-Smith *Judahite Burial Practices and Beliefs about the Dead* (Sheffield, JSOT Press; 1992).

10. Tamar in Gen. 38 is claiming her rights under this law and it is alluded to in the story of Ruth, where her kinsman has a prior claim on her over Boaz (Ruth 4.6). The sanction outlined in Deut. 25.9–10 against the one who fails in this duty is the fitting one that his family will be henceforth remembered as the 'house of him that had his sandal pulled off' – a reference to the right of the outraged widow to pull off his sandal and spit in his face in front of the elders.

11. The argument for a relationship between ancient Near Eastern culture and the development of patriarchal structures is set out forcibly in Gerda Lerner's *The Creation of Patriarchy* (Oxford, OUP; 1986), especially chapters 8 and 9. An intriguing discussion that develops on similar lines to the present one is to be found in D. Young's *Origins of the Sacred: The Ecstasies of Love and War* (London, Abacus; 1993) pp. 74–112. Young gives an anthropological account of the evolution of love as a precarious mechanism for binding the male into the rearing of children. The precariousness of

this may only too easily allow the eruption of anger and ultimately of murder into the family situation.

12. A useful survey of this debate which itself concludes that such a cult was a legitimate part of Israel's worship until the Deuteronomic reforms in G.C. Heider *The Cult of Molek: A Reassessment* (Sheffield JSOT Press; 1985).

13. Zech. 13:3.

14. For a survey and commentary on this literature see H.E. Goldin *Hebrew Criminal Law and Procedure* (New York, Twayne Publishers Inc.; 1952) pp. 166–175.

15. Tractate Sanhedrin 71a. See H. Danby *Tractate Sanhedrin: Mishnah and Tosefta* (London, SPCK; 1919) p. 107.

16. See Hosea 13.4–16; 5.14. The fact these passages are counterbalanced by others in the book which speak of forgiveness and restoration is not strictly relevant to this argument. These destructive emotions and threats are not represented as idle bluster on God's part, whatever else may be said about them.

17. See also the parallel in Matt. 10.37–38, which does not use the word 'hate', but rather speaks of the need to love Jesus more than mother and father. This is scandal enough. The issues as to why the two versions differ are too convoluted to go into here. The mere fact that Luke records the tradition in the way cited is sufficient witness to this strand in the New Testament.

18. See also the parallels in Matt. 12.46–50; Luke 8.19–21.

19. One could even argue that the fact that Luke feels constrained to conclude his account of Jesus' youthful escapade in the temple, where he disappears without his parents' leave and where he explicitly alludes to the prior claim of his heavenly father on his time, with the note that on his return to Nazareth 'he was obedient to them' (Luke 2.51) is an indication that this charge of disobedience had already occurred to people.

20. Mark 12.18–27; Matt. 22.23–33; Luke 20.27–38.

21. The only place in which the Hebrew Scriptures allude to celibacy or at least abstinence as a virtue is in the context of the requirement for soldiers on active service to refrain from sexual activity. David pledges that his men have not touched a woman when he requests the bread from the altar at Nob (1 Sam. 21.4), and Uriah makes this custom the basis for his refusal to sleep with his wife Bathsheba when David recalls him from the front (2 Sam. 11.11). The otherwise anomalous celibacy of the Qumran community, if this was indeed their practice, can be related to their self-image as warriors prepared for the apocalyptic battle. There are suggestive pointers here to possible parallels in the practice of the early church. The attitude of the rabbinic tradition appears in passages such as this from the Talmud: 'The sages in the school of R. Ishmael taught: "Until a young man reaches the age of twenty, the Holy One sits and waits expectantly: 'When will this one take a wife?' But when a young man reaches the age of twenty and has still not wed, He says, 'May the bones of this one be blasted.'"' (B. Kid 29b–30a). The rabbis also drew on the story of Adam and Eve to show that man only achieves completeness as part of a couple (e.g. B. Yev 63a).

22. The relevant passages are Mark 10.2–12; Matt 19.1–9; Luke 16.18. The well-known concession over the woman's adultery which appears in Matt 19.9 may itself show a developing awareness of the consequences of an absolute ban and clearly reflects the continuing need to control women's sexuality.

23. See *inter alia* Isa. 44.9–20; 46.1–7; 2.12–22.

24. R.P. Carroll *Wolf in the Sheepfold: The Bible as a Problem for Christianity* (London, SPCK; 1993)

3

THE FAMILY IN THE EARLY CHURCH

Frances Young

In the second century, they used to tell the story of Thecla. An Asian presbyter, 'for love of Paul'[1] we are told, collected this and other stories and wrote them down in a book called *The Acts of Paul*. Paul was in flight from Antioch and at Iconium he was met and received by someone called Onesiphoros, whose household, by the way, is greeted twice in 2 Timothy on the grounds that he had supported Paul in prison.

At the house of Onesiphoros, according to the *Acts of Paul*,[2] there was an assembly of Christians, with 'great joy and bowing of knees and breaking of bread, and the word of God concerning continence and the resurrection', as Paul said (amongst other things):

Blessed are the pure in heart, for they shall see God.
Blessed are they who have kept the flesh pure, for they shall become a temple of God.
Blessed are the continent, for to them the Lord will speak.
Blessed are they who have wives as they had them not, for they shall inherit God.
Blessed are the bodies of virgins, for they shall be well pleasing to God and shall not lose the reward of their purity . . .

Now as Paul addressed the congregation in the house of Onesiphoros, 'a virgin named Thecla . . . sat at a nearby window and listened night and day to the word of virgin life as it was spoken by Paul; and she did not turn away from the window, but pressed on in the faith rejoicing exceedingly'. The story goes on to explain how deeply she desired to be counted worthy of joining the group. From the perspective of the storyteller, her subsequent adventures following Paul confirmed her sainthood, and in the fourth century, the pilgrim Egeria[3] tells of a

29

visit to her shrine and of the commemorative reading there of
The Acts of Paul and Thecla.

The second century story-teller, however, is skilled enough
to be able to adopt a different voice in the narrative. When
Thecla is introduced, he or she notes that her mother was
Theocleia and that she was betrothed to a man named
Thamyris. Family lineage is thus marked up as an issue. Sure
enough, Thecla's obsession with sitting at the window listening
to Paul drove her mother to send for Thamyris, and he 'came
in great joy as if he were already taking her in marriage'. On
arrival, he bursts out, 'Where is my Thecla, that I may see her?'
Theocleia tells a tale of woe: for three days and three nights
Thecla has not got up from the window either to eat or to
drink. She clearly has a crush on this strange man who teaches
deceptive and subtle words. The offending doctrines concern
a single God and living chastely.

Despite her modesty – Thecla has clearly been brought up to
be a dutiful daughter, living in seclusion, awaiting her arranged
marriage, thus showing the standard maidenly virtues of the
time – she appears to her mother as:

> . . . like a spider at the window bound by his words, . . . dominated
> by a new desire and a fearful passion; for the maiden hangs upon
> the things he says and is taken captive.

Thamyris is sent to reason with her. Her mother cannot keep
back from the encounter.

> And those who were in the house wept bitterly, Thamyris for the
> loss of a wife, Theocleia for that of a daughter, the maidservants
> for that of a mistress. So there was a great confusion of mourning
> in the house. And while this was going on [all around her] Thecla
> did not turn away, but gave her whole attention to Paul's word.

We will leave our story there and pause to reflect on its significance for our theme. The first thing to observe is that we are
not dealing with a society made up of nuclear families with 2.4
children in 2.5 bedrooms. To imagine ourselves into the story
we need to recall something like Jane Austen or the television
show *Upstairs Downstairs*: the household is a whole mini-
society, with servants and slaves as well as the extended kinship

group, and ensuring the proper inheritance of property by appropriate marriage alliances is a vital family concern.

However, the most striking thing is that early Christianity is not perceived here as upholding family values; rather, it tends to be subversive of the family. The preaching of chastity, celibacy or virginity was a radical challenge to then contemporary society, whether pagan or Jewish. The story of Thecla throwing over all her opportunities in life (in other words, a good marriage) – behaving in a very unwomanly manner, visiting Paul in prison, condemned to be burnt on a public pyre but saved by a providential thunderstorm, rejoining Paul but arrested in Antioch and thrown to the wild beasts, though baptising herself as she faced them and then miraculously delivered, finally donning the cloak of a philosopher and becoming a teacher like Paul – this story held out a model of the Christian life for women which some might see as liberating, others as dangerously disruptive – disruptive of society because disruptive of the family.

There would seem to be several themes to be taken up and the rest of this discussion will be shaped accordingly. First we will sketch normal expectation about families and households in Greco-Roman society; and then we will consider the various ways in which Christians sought to be obedient to their traditions within that social setting. In both cases, we will be focusing on the 'ideologies' involved – for we know more about that from ethical treatises than we do about actual practice. Finally, we will glance at Christian family life as found particularly in the literature of the fourth century. Here the ambivalences remain but are, if I may hazard an all too appropriate metaphor, 'domesticated'. There emerged a standard church view delicately balancing the merits of domestic bliss and monastic devotion, though somewhat to the detriment of the former. For women, Mary provided a present model of ideal motherhood or perpetual virginity (if not both), but in Paradise there were assuredly no cities, professions, houses or even marriage, for virginity was and will be the perfect life. Jesus told us, after all, that in the resurrection 'they shall neither marry nor give in marriage, but they shall be like the angels' (Matt. 22.30).[4]

Greco-Roman Society and the Household

We are walking down a street in more or less any city around the Mediterranean in more or less any century between the second BCE and the fourth CE. You can get something of the feel of it by visiting Pompeii. To twentieth century western eyes, the biggest surprise would be the fact that among the crowds in the public spaces of the city, there are precious few women. We are guests invited to the house of Marcus, a wealthy merchant, for an afternoon of philosophical conversation with a visiting teacher.

As we pass from the street across the threshold, we move into private space. We are taken across the courtyard and shown into a cool room decorated with mosaic and wall-paintings, a room where visitors are received. This may be private territory, but there is this semi-public area reserved for the leisure and business of the usually male head of the household.

We will almost certainly not be invited to meet his wife and children who will be in seclusion in the truly private part of the house. It is a matter of pride that his wife does not have to work outside the home, or even go shopping – there are plenty of servants to do that, indeed we will be waited on by servants who probably have the status of slaves. In terms of legal status, the women and minors will be little better off – all are in some sense the property of the head of the household.[5]

The philosopher whom we have come to hear is one of those Cynics[6] who live off their patrons, stimulating them with rather shocking moral teaching about the vanity of life and its concerns while never demanding any real sacrifice from their hearers. They do parrot the old ethical traditions, however, well known since Plato and Aristotle. The household is the mirror of society, and each household head should be a bit like a philosopher-king. If he cannot keep his household in order, how can he expect to be effective in leadership in the wider world?

For all that, within the private space of the home, it is likely that his wife reigns supreme. After all, Marcus is mainly concerned with business and public affairs and it is a matter of pride that he made a good marriage. Obtaining a wife from a family that could further his business alliances had been a priority, of course, the principal point of marriage being the production of sons and heirs (that, by the way, means the disposal of any unwanted children, babies with defects, excess daughters);[7] but it is also important that she had the gifts and training to manage his establishment and that in this they have common goals, she representing him in the daily dealing of the household.

Of course, to protect her reputation, she is required to have a servant in attendance at all times, and to conduct business from the house. Religious rites and festivals provide one of the few reasons why she leaves the house. It simply is not done for a respectable married woman to appear in public. Even so, she is able to exercise quite a bit of patronage, supporting financially projects that interest her.

In the end, legal status is not much indication of power or authority. One problem in the household is the tension between two influential people, Marcus's wife and the *oikon-omos*,[8] or steward. The household is not merely a consumer unit, but a production unit. This is not one of the great land-owning households, but rather a trading family, ship-owners, importers and exporters, and in fact Marcus allows both his wife and his freedman-steward to own property and carry on their own business transactions.

Apart from being an economic entity, the household is itself a religious unit. There is a shrine to the gods which protect it, and all members of the household, slave as well as free, are under their protection. Each day rites are performed, and from generation to generation the family obligations include remembering the dead and practising the traditional customs. Births and deaths were matters of household rituals, and children were assimilated into their parent's religious habits. On her marriage, the wife would have transferred allegiance to the gods of her household, as would newly acquired slaves.

The picture just created is inevitably a set of generalisations. Some variations in the legal status of women can be documented from place to place and century to century, but generally speaking *mutatis mutandis* this picture would be a reasonable sketch for Greek, Roman and Jewish households, and would be replicated in Spain, Syria, Egypt and elsewhere.[9]

The trouble is, of course, that it is built up of a combination of literary, legal and archaeological data, the literary material largely reflecting conditions among high-class landowners rather than urban merchants. Furthermore, it tells us little about the family life of slaves, the poor or the dwellers in the *insulae* – the blocks of flats which were certainly a feature of Italian cities and probably elsewhere. It is likely that the poor, slaves and freedmen had great difficulty in establishing stable family lives at all – in fact, non-citizens could not legally marry and slave children belonged to the owner of the mother. But there are genuine hints in the evidence available of real family affection, as well as the occasionally family feud, at all levels of society. For Plutarch, that prolific Greek essayist of the first century CE (Common Era), the seeds of all social virtues are found 'in the joy we have in our children and out love of them, emotions which accompany their first beginnings.'[10]

Early Christianity and the family

Now let us suppose that this typical house is in Corinth in the first century CE and when we get to the meeting we find a funny little Jew called Paul pretending to be a philosopher.[11] It seems that he is carrying on just like the Cynics, making the same claims to have the truth and put the world to rights. What he has to say we find intriguing and we get invited to attend some gathering at another house. It must be some sort of *collegium* we suppose – a club or association.

When we get to this meeting, we are quickly astonished to find that it includes all the women and children, slaves and servants of the household where it is held, as well as many outsiders. Even more extraordinary is the fact that they are all calling each other 'brother' and 'sister', and there are quite a lot of elderly men and women who are treated as if honoured parents.[12] The head of the household seems to open his doors to the group as if he were the patron of a *collegium*, and his steward seems to be responsible for seeing that attendants (*diakonoi*) get things ready for the gathering, but the host apparently does not have control over what happens in the meeting. The central feature seems to be the typical *collegium* dinner-party, but with all the women and children present, it is more like a grand family meal, though there is also the psalm-singing, scripture readings and ethical talks like you would have if you visited a synagogue. We are not sure whether to treat this as a public or private occasion.[13]

The striking thing this Paul is saying is that the God and King of the universe, the God worshipped by the Jews, has adopted non-Jews into his family. Of course, it is a universal commonplace that God is Father of all, and adoption is a common enough thing, especially when a father has not succeeded in producing a suitable adult son as his heir. But this seems a bit odd: God is presented as the Father of a true Son, Jesus Christ, and by being baptised into this Christ, anyone can be adopted as son of God and heir of God's promises. Even these women and children, slaves and servants become sons and heirs when baptised into this group.[14] This is not just philosophy after all – it apparently involves joining an alternative family.[15]

This alternative family is supposed to anticipate the kingdom of God. That is not so different, we suppose, from the philosophical teaching that households should be run like mini states, but it is dangerous politically. These people are even claiming to be aliens and strangers here on earth[16] and expecting people to give up their traditional customs, ready for some great denouement when this Jesus will return as God's chief minister of state.

Now what happens to normal family values when loyalty to an alternative takes over? Surprisingly, the more we listen to this Paul the more we realise how conservative – indeed Jewish – he is in his ideas about respectable and decent behaviour.[17] He is not too keen on the wilder tendencies evident in the group – the tongue-speaking and prophesying, especially the women who get out of control and let their hair down in public. There are real hierarchies in this 'household of God', too, just like any other household, and actually these Christians are a bit two-faced. One minute they are talking about being part of God's family, next minute we are all supposed to be the slaves and servants of God.

In fact, obedience seems to be the chief virtue around here, and the family language is all mixed up with terms of servitude: What officials there are are called *episkopoi* and *diakonoi*[18] – in other words, gangs of servants with their foremen or overseers. Paul himself takes a pride in being the slave of Christ acting as his 'letter-carrier' or messenger – a mere *apostolos* or *diakonos*, bearing the authority and seal of his master, like an *oikonomos* or steward.[19] Altogether we feel a bit confused by it all, but we cannot deny the excitement and the tensions in this novel community.

Having embarked on this imaginary visit, the temptation is to go on developing it. But it is important for our purposes to step back a little and to move forward in time. The Pauline communities we meet in the authentic letters were bound to struggle with the ambivalences our sketch has brought out. Here were the seeds of radicalism, and the roots of a reaction back to socially acceptable norms – if only for the sake of proclaiming the gospel in that society. The key point, however, is this: attitudes to the family in the early church are ineradicably bound up with the very nature of the church itself.

Radical alternatives and their motivation

Now one thing is quite clear: the earliest Christian communities, Paul included, believed that the end of the world was upon them. In this perspective, the ordinary business and relationships of life tended to appear in a different light. In his letters to Corinth, Paul assures his 'brothers' in the community that the time will not last long and that the world as we know it is passing away (1 Cor. 7.29, 31). That being the case, the best thing is for each to remain in their existing situation through the time of crisis: a slave is the Lord's freedman, and every free man who has received the call is a slave of Christ, but that does not mean changed status here and now, any more than a Jew should seek to remove the mark of circumcision. The married belong to each other and should stay that way, the unmarried should also stay as they are, unless they have insufficient self control; the advantage of singleness is being able to concentrate on the Lord's business rather than being pulled in two directions, and that applies to both men and women.

Earlier in the letter Paul has spoken of the importance of sexual purity, since the bodies of the faithful are temples of the Holy Spirit. It is not hard to see how Paul's caution and conventionalism could easily be over-ruled, and it is quite clear that the motivation for the celibacy or virginity of Thecla and those who regarded her as a hero was related to this kind of eschatological perspective. Chastity was required because of the expectation of bodily resurrection, and the need to be pure for the life of the world to come: in the *Acts of Thecla*, Paul is accused of saying, 'Otherwise there is no resurrection for you, except you remain chaste and do not defile the flesh, but keep it pure', and the accusation is made by others named Demas and Hermogenes who claim they will teach about a resurrection 'which has already taken place in the children whom we have, and that we are risen again in that we have come to know the true God'. As in the Johannine epistles, these 'children' may be metaphorical – their followers or converts, and it would seem here that there is a hint of the struggle between two kinds of radical which had emerged in the second century, the encratites and the gnostics.[20]

To cut a long story short, whereas the encratites wanted to keep the body pure for the coming millennial kingdom, the gnostics had lost interest in the unfulfilled prediction of a new heaven and a new earth, and they taught that the body (*soma*) was a tomb (*sema*). They found release in their spirits, the sparks of the divine which had become enmeshed in this alien material world, but which were already redeemed through knowledge of their true spiritual nature. For both groups, normal social relations and the everyday business of life ceased to matter. Strict asceticism accompanied women's liberation from the chains of domesticity and childbirth. Like Thecla, they became prophets and martyrs, belonging only to Jesus Christ, his betrothed virgins. Or as Gnostics, they transcended their female bodies: the gospel of Thomas reported that when 'Simon Peter said to them "Mary should leave us, for females are not worthy of life", Jesus said, "See, I am going to attract her to make her male so that she too might become a living spirit that resembles you males. For every (female) element that makes itself male will enter the kingdom of heaven".'[21]

Either way presupposes a radical attitude towards family life and Hugh Pyper's discussion in this volume shows how the potential for this development was there in the biblical tradition. It is not altogether surprising to find in the apocryphal *Acts of Thomas* the story of a young couple on their bridal night having a vision of Christ which prevents them consummating their marriage! If they abandon 'filthy intercourse', they will become 'holy temples, pure and free from afflictions and pains both manifest and hidden', and they will 'not be girt about with cares for life and for the children, the end of which is destruction.'[22]

The rejection of extremism

But that kind of extremism was increasingly marginalised and indeed associated with heresy.[23] It was the conservative instincts of Paul which prevailed in the Christian mainstream. They were enshrined in the developing canon of Paul's writings. Already in Colossians (3.18ff), probably Paul himself had adopted the tone of the Cynic teachers, mapping out proper behaviour in the Christian household according to the traditional patterns: the relations of husband and wife, father and children, master and slaves. In Ephesians 5.21–6.9, someone, probably not Paul himself, but one of his followers, elaborated this with more specifically Christian warrants for the structures of obedience and love; as the church is subject to Christ, so must wives be subject to their husbands, and as the church is loved by Christ, so must husbands love their wives. Children must obey their parents and slaves give obedient and cheerful service; on the other hand, fathers are not to provoke resentment in their children, but bring them up in the discipline and instruction of the Lord, and masters must remember that they have the same master in heaven and there is no favouritism there.[24]

Probably after Paul's death, the churches that saw him as their authority developed these old household codes into primitive church canons, codes for God's household, the alternative family. These we find in the so-called pastoral epistles, 1 & 2 Timothy and Titus, and it is a hard job deciding where the old family categories have turned into ecclesiastical offices.[25] There are 'seniors' or 'elders', 'presbyters' who have to be respected rather like families' grandparents, and having long memories are given some kind of teaching authority; but they also, apparently, constitute some kind of governing council. There are 'widows' whose status is much debated: do they constitute some kind of order of celibates with ministerial functions, or are they just older members of the community who are given charitable support by the congregation? The 'foreman' or *episkopos* is clearly in charge, and he's supposed to be a respectable head of household, able to control his own establishment or he is not fit to run the church. There are also manservants and also, it would seem, maidservants (or female deacons), but whether they would have the same duties is questionable. They presumably would not have in most households.

But fascinating as these questions are, we must move on, simply noting that features such as the advice on the conduct of worship, or the injunctions to widows with children not to expect church support, suggest a developing structure of church life which upholds rather than provides substitutes for normal family life. Both church structures and household hierarchies betray current patriarchal assumptions, and there is no radical challenge to existing social norms. Women are put in their place, and told they are saved by child-bearing! (1 Tim 2.11–15).

All this is further evidenced in the so-called Apostolic Fathers. Clement of Rome, writing to the Corinthians in the 90s, commends them:

> For your elders were treated with the honour due to them; your young men were counselled to be soberly and seriously minded; your womenfolk were bidden to go about their duties in irreproachable devotion and purity of conscience, showing all proper affection to their husbands; they were taught to make obedience the rule of their lives, to manage their households decorously, and to be patterns of discretion in every way.[26]

Polycarp, a generation later, echoes the pastoral epistles in regulating widows, and speaking of instructing 'our womenfolk in the traditions of the faith, and in love and purity; teaching them to show fondness and fidelity to their husbands, and a chaste and impartial affection for everyone else, and to bring up their children in the fear of God'.[27]

Such traditions are incorporated and developed in the *Apostolic Constitutions*, a church manual gradually compiled over the first few centuries. We will not delay by repeating the regulations concerning celibate women, widows and virgins, the apparent clamping down on ministerial activities like baptising, the exhortations to wives. Rather let us note what is said about children.[28] Fathers were to educate children in the Lord, teach them appropriate trades (some were banned for Christians), and not be afraid to reprove them. Extensive quotations from the book of Proverbs reinforce the advice to discipline them (e.g. Prov. 13.24): 'he that spareth the rod hateth his son'! Young people are not to be allowed to club together with their equals and when they reach the right age for marriage, proper arrangements are to be made so that they do not 'in the heat and fervour of their age' get tempted into sexual adventures[29] for which parents will have to give an account on the Day of Judgment.

If it all seems harsh to us, it was then normal – indeed beneficent. What is striking is another section where it is suggested that:

> When any Christian becomes an orphan, whether it be a young man or a maid, it is good that some one of the brethren without a child should take the young man, and esteem him in place of a son; and he that has a son about the same age and that is marriageable, should marry the maid to him: for they do so perform a great work, and become fathers to orphans, and shall receive the reward of this charity from the Lord God.[30]

Christian love could still over-ride the conventional need for the family, child-bearing and marriage alliances to ensure the future of property. And the total ban on contraception and abortion found in traditional Christianity dates from Christian opposition to the treatment of human reproduction as principally to do with property rights rather than God's gift of life to each individual creature.[31] So too the moral disapproval of exposing infants: once conceived they should be reared and the only birth control should be the control of passion. The church may have taken over the family values of the Greco-Roman world, but it was not without significant critique.

Fourth Century Christian Life

By the fourth century, imperial patronage ensured that upper class families were attracted to Christianity, and that bishops were increasingly drawn from local aristocrats. There is, I fear, too little space to explore many of the intriguing examples to be found in the more abundant literature of this period.[32] In the East, the literary endeavours and personal correspondence of the Cappadocian Fathers reveals a good deal about their family relationships: Gregory of Nazianzus composed funeral orations for his father, brother and sister while Gregory of Nyssa made his sister Macrina the chief character in philosophical dialogues. Here we glimpse the ideals of wifely virtues and of ascetic withdrawal, lived out on the family estates. In the west, Augustine describes his childhood in the first autobiography ever to be written, his *Confessions*, and lifts the curtain on his relationship with his mother.

Jerome corresponds with women who, having done their duty in raising heirs, adopt a celibate life, often travelling to Egypt and Palestine to visit monastic heroes in the desert.[33] In this circle of upper-class Roman women, we find some who, with their elite education, gain reputations for scholarship and wisdom, others with financial independence, who found and endow monasteries. So a working compromise between family pressures and radicalism is achieved.

Yet the price of the inheritance from early Christianity is found in the contradictions between Jerome's theologically grounded misogyny and his admiration for these saintly women who are his patrons. It is perhaps significant that whereas a good deal of advice is found on the education of sons in ancient literature, it is in Jerome's correspondence that we find advice on the education of daughters,[34] and this provides snapshots of family life that we can scarcely pass over.

To take one instance, the granddaughter and namesake of Paula, Jerome's most important patron, is already dedicated to the life of a virgin and her education must be fitting for one who is to be a temple of the Lord. No filthy words or lustful boys are to get near and even her women in waiting are to be protected from the world. She should play with toy letters, and keep them in order by using an alphabetic rhyme. Her hand can be guided as she tries to write her first letters. Rewards for spelling are fine and she ought to have friends learning with her to provide competition. She is to learn the Scriptures, in Latin and Greek, and to acquire a love of Christian books, not for their rich bindings but their contents. She may be educated but her life will be restricted entirely to the private domestic sphere, it seems.

The family as private institution

And that brings us conveniently back to the fundamental point about the family – the fact that ancient life was customarily organised in two spheres: public affairs and private matters. Both public affairs and private matters, as John Chrysostom tells us in a homily on the kind of women to be taken as wives, were determined by God:

> To woman is assigned the presidency of the household; to man all the business of state, the marketplace, the administration of justice, government, the military and all other such enterprises. A woman is not able to hurl a spear or shoot an arrow, but she can grasp the distaff, weave at the loom; she correctly disposes of all such tasks that pertain to the household. She cannot express her opinion in a legislative assembly, but she can express it at home, and often she is more shrewd about household matters than her husband. She cannot handle state business well, but she can raise children correctly, and children are our principal wealth. At a glance she can detect the bad behaviour of the servants and manage them carefully. She provides complete security for her husband and frees him from all such household concern, concerns about money, woolworking, the preparation of food and decent clothing . . . Indeed, this is a work of God's love and wisdom, that he who is skilled at the greater things is downright inept and useless at the performance of the less important ones, so that the woman's service is necessary . . . Let us thus strive for just one goal, virtue of soul and nobility of behaviour, so that we may enjoy peace, live in concord and maintain ourselves in love unto the end.[35]

The domestication of Christian family values according to the norms of ancient Greco-Roman society has lasted a long time, and its price had been the seclusion of women in the private sphere. Might there be some other resolution of the tension between the values of society and Christian radicalism? In a totally different social setting, the answer must surely be 'Yes' and must surely not be simply the reaffirmation of those Greco-Roman norms, despite their long-standing baptism into Christ.

NOTES

1. Tertullian, *De Baptismo*, p. 17.

2. *Acts of Paul and Thekla* 4–7 in W. Hennecke, *New Testament Apocrypha II*, ed. R. McL. Wilson (London, Lutterworth; 1965), pp. 345ff.

3. *The Pilgrimage of Egeria* 23.5, in *Ancient Christian Writers*; excerpts in Clark E. A. *Women in the Early Church* [Message of the Fathers of the Church vol. 13] (Wilmington DL, Michael Glazier Inc; 1983); see p. 192.

4. John Chrysostom *On Virginity*, and Jerome *Against Jovinian*, in Clark *Women*: pp. 122–131.

5. In creating the picture offered in these paragraphs I am especially indebted to the material assembled in David C. Verner *The Household of God: The Social World of the Pastoral Epistles* [SBL Dissertation Series 71] (Chico CA, Scholars Press; 1983) and Karen Jo Torjesen *When Women were Priests: Women's Leadership in the Early church and the Scandal of their Subordination in the Rise of Christianity* (San Francisco, Harper; 1993); both I have used freely, and compounded with those other sources acknowledged in the notes.

6. See Abraham Malherbe's collection of papers published under the title *Paul and the Popular Philosophers* (Minneapolis, Fortress Press; 1989).

7. Sarah B. Pomeroy, 'Infanticide in Hellenistic Greece' in Cameron and Kuhrt *Images* p. 207–222, tries to estimate the extent to which this well-known fact actually affected the ratio of males to females in the population.

8. For this paragraph, see Dale B. Martin *Slavery as Salvation: The Metaphor of Slavery in Pauline Christianity* (New Haven NJ, Yale University Press; 1990).

9. For a comprehensive gathering of data for a later period, see Clark *Women*. She stresses in the conclusion (p. 140) that the basic domestic expectations inherited from earlier centuries seem more or less unchanged for the majority of women.

10. Plutarch *Moralia VI: De amore prolis* 3, 495c (Loeb edn): p. 342. The sketch above can be filled out from Plutarch's essays: he wrote a *Consolatio* (Loeb edn, vol VII, p. 580ff.) for his wife on the death of their two year old daughter which indicates both familial affection and the usual use of nursemaids in aristocratic households. It also indicates both the expected simplicity and seclusion of a woman's life and her public appearance on the occasion of religious festivals. In his essay on the education of children (cited above), he indicates that as far as means allow, even people of less affluence should endeavour to follow the same advice.

11. Malherbe, *Paul*, developed the position of E.A. Judge that Paul was more like a sophist than anything else. For the perspectives of this section, see also his 'House

44   THE CHRISTIAN FAMILY

Churches and their Problems' in *Social Aspects of Early Christianity* [2nd edn] (Philadelphia Fortress; 1983): pp. 60–91.

12. *Adelphoi*, and occasionally its feminine form are used in Acts and the Epistles *passim*; especially note 1 Tim 5.2 for the 'parental' relationship.

13. This ambiguity is increasingly seen as lying at the root of the problems concerning women's leadership in the church. See Torjesen *When Women were Priests* ch. 2; Kraemer R.S. *Her Share of the Blessings: Women's Religions among Pagans, Jews and Christians in the Greco-Roman World* (New York, OUP; 1992) p. 142; and Wire A. *Corinthian Women Prophets* (Minneapolis, Fortress; 1990) p. 183.

14. Rom. 8.14; Gal. 3.26–4.7, 4.21–5.1.

15. In the Acts of the Apostles, the emergent community of Christians comprises a new voluntary association that in many ways replaces the family and community its members have left (Kraemer *Her Share*: p. 141).

16. Phil. 3.20; 1 Peter 2.11.

17. In 1 Corinthians, Paul takes a generally conventional Jewish line on sexual ethics, going to law, eating idol-meat, etc. as well as trying to bring order into Christian meetings in chapters 11 and 14.

18. Phil 1.1 alone among the probably authentic Pauline letters uses this term, though see Rom. 16.1 where Phoebe is described as *diakonos* and Col. 4.7 where Tychicus is described as *adelphos* and *diakonos*. The problem is that Paul uses the term diakonos of himself (e.g. 2 Cor. 3, similarly Eph. 3.7) so that it cannot always have a technical sense. By the time of the Pastorals, both terms are clearly used of church offices.

19. For further amplification, see Dale Martin, *Slavery*.

20. For further information and bibliography, see Frances Young *The Theology of the Pastoral Letters* (Cambridge, CUP; 1994).

21. Layton B. *The Gnostic Scriptures* (London, SCM Press Ltd; 1987): p. 399.

22. Acts of Thomas I:12; ET in Hennecke *New Testament Apocrypha* II: p. 449.

23. See 'Heresy as Women's Religion: Women's Religion as Heresy' ch. 11 of Kraemer *When Women were Priests*: pp. 157–173.

24. Cf. also 1 Peter 2.18–3.7 On the apologetic use of *Haustafeln* see Malherbe *Social Aspects*: p. 52ff. For discussion see Verner *Household*.

25. For a full discussion see Frances Young *Theology of the Pastoral Epistles*.

26. *1 Clement* 1; in *Early Christian Writings*, trans. Staniforth M. rev. w. intro. Louth A. (London, Penguin Classics: 1989) p. 23.

27. *Early Christian Writings*: p. 120.

28. *Apostolic Constitutions* IV:11; *Ante-Nicene Christian Library* vol 17.

29. Plutarch gives the same advice – to curb young men by marrying them off and so preventing sexual adventures; *On the education of children* 19 (Loeb edn): p. 64.

30. Apostolic Constitutions IV:1.

31. See Augustine 'On Marriage and Concupiscence' I: 15, 17 in Clark *Women*: p. 58). In defending marriage, particularly under the pressures of the fourth century ascetic movement, the Fathers treated it as a God-given arrangement for procreation though Austine also treats as 'good' in marriage 'fidelity and the sacramental bond'. See further other passages collected by Clark. Chrysostom makes it clear that riches and property are not a good reason for marrying (Clark *Women*: p. 36). See the

discussion of contraception, abortion and exposure (Clark *Women* esp. ch. 3). For the usual view of marriage and family as pertaining to property rights, see Countryman L.W. *Dirt Greed and Sex: Sexual Ethics in the New Testament and their Implication for Today* (London, SCM Press; 1989).

32. See Clark G. *This Female Man of God: Women and Spiritual Power in the Patristic Age, AD 350–450* (London, Routledge; 1995).

33. Clark *Women* provides a useful collection of material. See also her *Ascetic Piety and Women's Faith: Essays on late Ancient Christianity* [Studies in Women and Religion p. 20] (Lewiston, Edward Mellem Press; 1986).

34. See Clark *Women*: pp. 168–172 for extracts quoted.

35. Clark *Women*: pp. 36–37.

4

VICTORIAN FAMILY VALUES

Alistair Mason

Any early Victorian parent wanting to instil family values was likely to turn to Mrs Sherwood.[1] Her books for children were best-sellers; she published more than 400 titles; and her fictional Fairchild family was in its day one of the most evocative names in England. People remembered having her works read to them.

The History of the Fairchild Family[2] is no longer in print. We would be likely to find it off-putting. In each little story the Fairchild children behave like children we have known. They bicker occasionally, they have little jealousies and sulks, when bored they get into mischief. It is on the level of one sister getting a new doll, and the other, when invited to play with it, doesn't want to know, because she didn't get one. They are certainly believable children, apart from being able to recite huge chunks of relevant Scripture, and one could quite imagine that Mrs Sherwood knew a lot about children, and could tell stories to them that would immediately hold their attention. But then, each time, after naughtiness that might, in a modern household, arouse little more than a rueful smile, the parents come in as the wrath of God. Every childish misdemeanour is treated as grave sin, and is explained to the child as evidence of the wicked corruption of human nature. There is the famous scene where Mr Fairchild, after a quarrel between the children, took them to see a gibbet, with a decaying corpse hanging in chains, as an object lesson of the penalties of the sin of Cain, who hated his brother.[3] The children, who are nice children, in each story realise their fault, shed bitter tears, and sincerely promise to amend. They are forgiven, kissed, and consoled. Family life is basically happy, but they learn some terrifying lessons on the way. I think the scene that frightened me most was when the children were taken to a house where someone had recently died.

> 'And will you please to go too, Master and Misses?' said the young woman, turning back to the children, who stood at the door. The children looked grave, and hung back a little while; at last Lucy stepped forward first, and the others followed. The young woman led them, through the lower room of the cottage, to a little door opening upon a narrow staircase. When they came to the door, they perceived a kind of disagreeable smell, such as they had never smelt before; this was the smell of the corpse, which having been dead now nearly two days, had begun to corrupt; and as the children went higher up the stairs, they perceived this smell more disagreeably.
>
> The body of the old man was laid out upon the bed in the upper room; the poor old wife, and Mr and Mrs Fairchild, with Mrs Goodwill, were sitting round the bed. The face of the corpse was quite yellow, there was no colour in the lips, the nose looked sharp and long, and the eyes were closed and sunk under the brow; the limbs of the corpse, stretched out upon the bed, and covered with a sheet, looked longer than is natural; and the whole appearance of the body was more ghastly and horrible than the children expected . . .[4]

Mr Fairchild then told them how death is the wages of sin, and prayed. Each little story ends with a prayer and a piece of religious verse, which Mrs Sherwood had selected to fit in with her theme. She provides, as it were, a little daily liturgy for children, a story, a prayer and a hymn. The prayer, which looks long on the page, takes less than two minutes to read aloud. Here is a typical one.

> O Almighty Father, who seest the hearts of all men, and their great corruption; Thou knowest we are not able of ourselves to keep Thy Commandments; no, nor even so much as to wish to keep them, unless Thou, O Lord, puttest that wish into our hearts. Hear the cry of a sinful child. We cannot count the number of times which we have broken Thy Commandments; not a day passes in which we do not offend Thee again and again. But, O Thou who sentest Thy dear Son to save poor sinners from hell! have mercy upon me, a poor wicked child; forgive my past wicked life, for the sake of the Lord Jesus Christ, who for my sake took upon Him the body of a man, and became my brother in the flesh, that

He might keep all Thy commandments, which no man but Himself was ever able to do. Oh, then, for this my dear Brother's sake, pardon my sins, Almighty Father, and for His dear sake, send Thy Holy Spirit into my heart, to cleanse my wicked heart, and to write Thy laws upon it, that I may henceforth keep Thy commandments, and lead a holy life. Hear the prayers of a poor sinful child, for Thy dear Son's sake, Jesus Christ our Lord.
Amen.[5]

You may still think that is too long.

Now it must be already obvious that I distrust Mr Fairchild's way of bringing up children, even if, and it is all true, his anger is predictable and explained, and he hugs them when they repent. When young Henry jibs at his first lesson in Latin, I know which one I identify with.

'Master Henry, why won't you learn your lesson? Is it so hard that you cannot?'

'Oh, no, John,' answered Henry; 'I could learn this first lesson if that were all, because papa has taught me how to pronounce the words! but if I learn this, I shall be made to try to learn the next, and so on through the book; and I am sure I cannot learn all the hard words in this book, and so I won't begin.'

'Oh, fie! Master Henry' . . .[6]

Henry has already been whipped; he is sent to Coventry by the entire household for this. It is as near an experience of hell for a child as Mrs Sherwood can devise. It seems to me that in these stories a great deal of negativity and aggression is directed towards children, which is cruel. Quite often, I suspect, people who want a return to Victorian family values are looking for a structured system for their own negativity and aggression towards children or women, and I do not want to encourage them.

However, we must not at once dismiss Victorian families as cruel to children on what we have just heard. I shall modify the picture, first with some history, then with some theology. First, Mrs Sherwood is a very *early* Victorian. She was born in 1775, an exact contemporary of Jane Austen, whom in occasional points of dry humour she resembles. They have moral rigour in common as well. The *History of the Fairchild Family* was first published in 1818, nearly twenty years before

Queen Victoria came to the throne. A gibbet was part of the bad old days to Victorians too. Early in the Queen's reign, Mrs Fairchild added two more volumes to the *History*, and these are visibly less frightening. Her theology had changed. Though the book remained in print into this century, Edwardian editions missed out the references to our general wickedness, all scenes that might keep a child awake at night, and indeed all calls to prayer.[7] Victorian family values changed. In the *History of the Fairchild Family* we can see one image of what they changed from. It is easy to find late Victorians whose reaction to the book was very like our own.

The family of sinners

Let us turn to Mrs Sherwoood's theology, the Evangelicalism that taught our sin and Christ's saving blood. Consider the subversive fact that we are *all* sinners, including Papa and Mama. In one of the early chapters of the book Mrs Fairchild tells the children the story of her own girlhood, brought up by two aunts. She goes into detail about how she used to torment the dog, and steal the sweets, frame the cat for breakages, and sit on the coachman's knee. But her picture of the aunts is even more telling.

'Then what did they teach you, mamma?' said Henry.

'Why, my dear,' answered Mrs Fairchild, 'almost the first things they taught me were the Ten Commandments; and they told me that they were the words of God; and that, if I did not keep these words I should go to hell, and be burnt in everlasting fire with the devil and his angels; but that, if I did keep these Commandments, I should go to heaven, and live with God and the holy angels for ever.'

'Why, my aunts could not keep the Commandments themselves,' said Lucy; 'because nobody can without the help of the Holy Spirit: and how could they expect you to do it, mamma, when you were a little girl?'

'My aunts,' said Mrs Fairchild, 'could not keep the Commandments any more than I did, my dear, that is true enough; but people who have not true religion often live for years, and even die, without knowing that they are sinners. The beginning of true religion, my dear, is to know that we are sinners.'

'Are my aunts dead?' said Henry.

'Yes, my dear,' said Mrs Fairchild.

'Then I am afraid that they are not gone to heaven,' said Henry.[8]

(The aunts had, in fact, had deathbed repentances). There we see a strenuous and stern upbringing, holding the fear of hellfire before the child, that nevertheless, according to Mrs Sherwood, has missed the point. There is no virtue in our own attempts at goodness, or in bullying children into being good. When she contrasts the Law and the Gospel, parental strictness is just as likely to be Law. Parents can be wrong. Some of Mrs Sherwood's most popular stories were of Christian children winning over unbelieving adults. The Fairchild children hear 'The account of a little boy, who, through God's grace, turned his parents to righteousness.[9] Mrs Sherwood was, in fact, an object of suspicion in her own day because in her stories, parents and those in authority were sometimes bad, or at least comic.[10] The Fairchild children might be told off for laughing at the little ways of visitors, but these little ways were so vividly described (I noted she resembled Jane Austen) that even a pious child would feel sympathy and understanding rather than deference. Mr Fairchild is rather a frightening figure, but I doubt if his sense of his own sin makes him more so. Consider the possibility that as parents lose their sense that we are all sinners, they become more pompous, more self-satisfied, and no less likely to seem demanding and oppressive to their children.

Is God our Father demanding and oppressive? My intention in this paper on religion and the family is to look primarily at how Victorians talked about God and Christ in family terms. It clearly reinforces the status of fathers in families that God is Father. There is poor little Henry Fairchild: 'The misery of those who are under the anger of God exemplified by the unhappiness of a child under the anger of his father.'[11] But a parent can be gracious. There is the story in Mrs Sherwood's Volume 2 of how the girls mocked an ugly visitor behind her back, and, being nice girls, were properly ashamed of themselves when she gave them a wonderful present. They told their mother, and to their great surprise, she didn't expect them to own up to the lady, or to sacrifice the presents.

'Oh mamma,' said Lucy, 'the more you talk, the more vexed I am with myself. What can I do? Shall I go and beg Miss Crosbie's pardon?' – 'Shall we, mamma?' added Emily.

'No, no, my children,' answered Mrs Fairchild, half smiling. 'What! would you give the poor lady pain by telling her wherefore you come to beg her pardon?'

'No,' replied Lucy thoughtfully, 'that will not do, I see.'

'But we will not wear our bonnets today, mamma,' said Emily, 'though it is so fine.'

'She wishes to see you in them,' answered their mamma: 'she must not be disappointed.'

'Mamma,' replied Lucy, 'will you then forgive us quite, and not punish us at all?'

'Why should I punish you?' asked Mrs Fairchild.

Lucy – 'Because we have been naughty.'

Mrs Fairchild – 'Do you wish to be punished, Lucy?'[12]

She goes on to explain to them that punishment is a deterrent. There is no mention of retribution. 'God loves you, and deals with you as dear children.' The voice of God is no longer the voice of inexorable law.

God as Victorian father

We turn from children's stories to theology for adults, but still on the question of Father and Son and inexorable law. The heart of the matter for evangelical Christians was that God the Son bore our sins upon the cross.

> There was no other good enough
> To bear the price of sin.

We had incurred the wrath of God the Father, and that wrath found its necessary outlet in the punishment of his Son in our place. In the nineteenth century this image of God as an angry Father came to worry people. They picked out strong phrases from evangelical sermons: 'It was wrath, all wrath; the Father loved to see him die', and said they were unworthy of God. This is a move from an understanding of Christ's saving work in terms of the verdict of a court of law to a change in a personal relationship. My present concern is to stress that family relationships are at stake. The Father loved the Son as a son;

and loves us as sons (– and daughters; but sonship is, we must hope, inclusive in the early Victorian theologians).

Consider John McLeod Campbell (1800–1872), a Scottish Presbyterian minister, who in 1831 was tried and convicted of heresy by the General Assembly of the Church of Scotland for being too keen on the fatherliness of God. The Assembly was split on another issue; this was the start of the Ten Years' Conflict leading to the Disruption; and neither side wanted to risk being tarred with heresy. As the century went on, the Scottish church felt a wrong had been done, and McLeod Campbell's book *The Nature of the Atonement* was a set book when I was a student in a Scottish divinity faculty.

McLeod Campbell stressed the fatherliness of God. The ultimate truth on which faith must rest is that God is our Father. That he sent his *Son* should tell us something. This is our family concern. It is not right here to assess how impersonal Calvinist orthodoxy was (probably less so than we think) but we can understand McLeod Campbell's concern. In a forensic theory of atonement . . .

> the confidence with which we may . . . think of ourselves as sons of God, and draw near to Him expecting to be acknowledged as such, is *no direct trust in a Father's heart at all, no trust in any feeling in God of which we are personally the objects as His OFF-SPRING,* but is in reality a trust in the *judicial grounds on which the title and place of sons is granted to us.*[13]

It is not by some legal fiction, or even valid papers of adoption, that we are children of God. The father falls on the neck of the prodigal son, and does not have to explain himself for doing so. This is what fathers are like. We should come to God like 'orphans who have found their long lost Father.'[14] It is an obvious family value that fathers should love their children; here is a Victorian theologian rubbing it in at the highest level. God deals with us as a perfect father would with naughty children.

> That God should by a miracle change a rebellious child into a loving child, would be no such glory to God, as that the knowledge of the fatherliness rebelled against, should, by virtue of the excellence inherent in that fatherliness, accomplish this result. 'We love Him because He first loved us.'[15]

God is grieved by our sin, not angry. 'There is much less spiritual apprehension necessary to the faith that God punishes sin, than to the faith that our sins do truly grieve God.' The image of God shifts from impersonal wrath to a grieving parent. Of course there are questions about how much better, if any, this is for the child. 'Mummy's not angry with you, she's just sad' – and the little monster goes away twisted with guilt. Nevertheless, McLeod Campbell is evidence of a new emotional intensity in Victorian fatherhood.

It had gone further by the end of the century. R.C. Moberly's book *Atonement and Personality* was published in 1900, the last year of the queen's reign. Moberly was not a Scottish heretic. He was an Anglican clergyman, the son of a high church bishop of Salisbury, and the book was written when he was Regius Professor of Pastoral Theology and Canon of Christ Church at Oxford. His son Sir Walter Moberly was also quite a distinguished theologian in his spare time.

This, then, was one of the great clerical families of England, and not merely clerical. There is a famous essay by Lord Annan on 'The intellectual aristocracy,'[16] about how nearly all the great men and women of eighteenth century are inter-related. This is nothing to do with the peerage, or even with money, but the highly civilised, the original thinkers, often come from quite a small number of families. The Moberlys are one of these families. So when R.C. Moberly is talking about the fatherliness of God, and about the skill with which God brings us up, we remember that his own father was a distinguished bishop and that his own children did well. This is not a world where fathers sleep in front of television sets. These Victorian fathers made a tremendous impact upon their children. It was not always a good one. If you want a darker story, find out what Archbishop Benson did to the psychology of his children.

God deals with us as children. Here is Moberly:

Think, then, of the attitude of a parent, patient, loving, and wise, in dealing with the naughtiness of a little child. The first thing which is obvious is that the parent loves the child anyhow. His whole treatment of the child . . . may be described, not unaptly, as the process of the wise diplomacy of love . . . with the first dim touch or gleam of child-like regret and sorrow, the love which was waiting, opens its arms as love . . . Love dare not, can not – being love – forgive in the height of the passion. Love dare not, can not – being love – fail to forgive, from the moment when forgiveness is possible . . . A child sent away for disobedience, offers shyly to come back. Is that shyness the wistful shyness of desire? or is it the awkward shyness of defiance? . . . It may be that mere wistfulness, if met with the open-armed embrace of forgiving love, will produce forthwith the faltering word of regret, or the tears without words, which are, so far, the little self's true effort of repudiation of sin, and of personal allegiance to righteousness.[17]

This is beautiful and subtle, and you can see how it is done. When I first read it, I felt it was far better than the old eighteenth-century language of 'breaking the child's will'. Now it does not seem to me so different from Mrs Sherwood. She would probably say it was identical. These are the thoughts in Mr Fairchild's head as he waits for Henry's repentance. When I think of theology, as opposed to child-rearing, as this is Moberly's account of the atonement, I am a little suspicious that anyone should picture the situation with himself so clearly in the divine role. A good father sees God in his own image.

He can know most of God, because it is through those family ties, and by those family names, that God reveals Himself to man, and reveals man's relations to Him. Fully to understand the meaning of a 'Father in Heaven' we must be fathers ourselves.[18]

That is not Moberly, it is Charles Kingsley, who wrote *The Water Babies*. As a book for children, *The Water Babies* is a step forward from Mrs Sherwood's books. Kingsley was another Anglican clergyman and professor. As we can see, he replaces 'Except ye become as little children' with 'except ye become fathers'. Modern intrusive biographers, explaining Kingsley's obvious anxieties about people remaining single, have told us all about his impressive sex drive. I think you deserve to be told more about what he was like as a father. Here is a specific example of Victorian family life.

Corporal punishment was never allowed. His own early experiences of the sense of fear and degradation it produced, of the antagonism it called out between child and parent, pupil and teacher, gave him a horror of it. 'Besides degrading both parties concerned,' he would say, 'it has other evils, for more than half the lying of children is, I believe, the result of fear, and the fear of punishment'. On these grounds, too, he made it a rule never to take a child suspected of a fault, at unawares, by sudden question or hasty accusation. 'Do *we* not,' he asked, 'pray daily, Lord, confound me not, and shall we dare to confound our own children by sudden accusation, or angry suspicion, making them give evidence against themselves, a thing which we don't allow a criminal to do in a court of law? The finer the nature . . . the more easily it is confounded. Suspicion destroys all confidence between parent and child' . . . Do you train a boy . . . by letting anger and punishment be the *first* announcement of his having sinned. If you do, you induce two bad habits; first, the boy regards his parent with a kind of blind dread, as a being who may be offended by actions which to *him* are innocent . . . Next, and worse still, the boy learns not to fear sin, but the *punishment* of it, and thus he learns to lie.[19]

I doubt if we are much advanced on that. Kingsley seems to have made a good father. We can presume that many fathers still were fierce unpredictable tyrants, like the wicked hypocrite Pontifex in Samuel Butler's *The Way of All Flesh*. You remember the story: the little boy couldn't pronounce the letter 'c'.

'Now, Ernest, I will give you one more chance, and if you don't say "come," I shall know that you are self-willed and naughty.'
A few minutes more and we could hear screams coming from the dining-room . . . and knew that poor Ernest was being beaten.
'I have sent him to bed,' said Theobald, as he returned to the drawing-room, 'and now, Christina, I think we will have the servants in to prayers,' and he rang the bell for them, red-handed as he was.[20]

But the possibility of there being loving fathers, and God being a loving father, in a way that we could understand loving, was there.

Jesus as brother

So far I have talked almost entirely about families in terms of fathers and children rather than husbands and wives. I suspect this is because I have been trying to drag in God. Victorian theologians wanted a more personal God. That works very well with God as a humane Father dealing with small children. But it makes for difficulty in using husband and wife metaphors.

Kingsley would risk: 'to know how Christ loved the Church, we must have wives to love, and love them,'[21] but it felt strained at the time. Revivalism, like Moody and Sankey, which had a sweet tooth and a taste for drawing-room ballads, sometimes depicted Christ as the believer's sweetheart –

> Closed in everlasting arms,
>   Pillowed on the loving breast . . .
> While he whispers in my ear
>   I am His, and He is mine![22]

but, as we all know, overt sexuality was uncommon in Victorian England, and even the metaphor of husband and wife was little used in theology.

So instead I continue with non-sexual family relationships, brothers and sisters. Remember Mrs Sherwood's prayer, in which Jesus is our brother: 'For my dear Brother's sake, pardon my sins'. She tended to see Jesus winning over an angry father,[23] but even the theologians of the fatherliness of God thought of brothers. McLeod Campbell once said: 'The light of truth in which I see God as my Father, is the light in which I see men as my brethren.'[24] Seeing men as brethren was not something new. The French Revolution wanted 'Liberty, equality, and *fraternity*', so talking about human brotherhood in the nineteenth century sounded political. I turn to a theologian with strong political links, F.D. Maurice (1805–72), one of the founders of Christian Socialism. Maurice was an Anglican clergyman, a professor who was put out of his chair for heresy, though once again the church has regretted this. His book *The Church a Family* (1850) overlaps with much that we have already touched on.

> Religious people suppose that every kind of effort must be used to make a child feel its sin, that so it may appreciate God's mercy in sending it a deliverer. I cannot but think that such a method has produced, and must produce, premature self-consciousness, then hypocrisy, then infidelity or despair.[25]
>   . . . I would simply ask, what a gospel from heaven can be, if it is not a gospel concerning a Father; if it is not a declaration how that Father looks upon His children, and what He has done to reconcile them to Himself.[26]

But what particularly struck me was how Maurice used the idea of brotherhood. There is politics there, not very left-wing politics, which does not surprise me, as I have read Maurice before: 'Some universal society must put itself forth substantially in the world. It may be one which extinguishes national and family life. It may be one which justifies all family and national life. It must be one or the other.'[27]

Communism is a threat to family life, Christianity (according to Maurice) justifies family life. So families come to grief without God, but God's chosen way of working is through families. Christ is our Elder Brother.

Let us think about elder brothers. The image is not an entirely positive one. If you were a boy with an elder brother, then he was likely to inherit the family estate, and you had to go out and make your fortune. If you were a girl, then your elder brother guarded the family's honour. I can think of Scottish ballads where the girl falls in love unsuitably and her brother kills her. In Victorian Britain, where there was a double standard in sex, brothers had expectations of their sisters.

> Must not every woman be somebody's sister, or at least somebody's daughter? . . . how can he be justified in treating any woman in a manner which, if practised towards his sister, would excite his unbounded indignation?[28]

That was a Presbyterian minister attacking the double standard. It reminds us that Victorian family values were up against some embarrassing facts.[29] Still, in Maurice's picture we see an elder brother as admirable, a real person and an intimate. And 'Must not the Elder Brother imply a Father'?[30] We come to God through Christ; we experience Christ as an elder brother. Here again are Victorian family values, where we meet Christ not as King or Redeemer or Saviour but as Brother.

Maurice, however, takes it further. The title of the book is *The Church a Family*. As I said, he affirms ordinary families, but the church is not an ordinary family. It is an ark full of strange beasts, who nevertheless are brothers and sisters. Because the church is a family looking up to an Elder Brother, 'the word *presbyter* (which means 'elder') almost inevitably offered itself as the earthly witness and counterpart of that truth.'[31] Whereas Professor Young seems to suggest that the titles of bishops and deacons come from overseers of slave estates, it is pleasantly surprising that the dull word 'presbyter' speaks to us of Christ our Elder Brother. This, I suspect, is a Victorian reading.

English Christianity in the nineteenth century liked talking of sisters and brothers. This was the age when England first saw Sisters of Mercy, and Sisters of the Poor. There were religious orders and parish fraternities. Not only high Anglicans but Free Churches had their sisterhoods. So, indeed, did hospitals, where a sister becomes a figure of authority. In practice this wider use of brother and sister probably undercuts ordinary family life. What seemed like a discovery of personal relationships became a new range of institutional titles. 'Father', at the same time, became a clerical title, slowly and against opposition within the Roman Catholic church, and as a badge of party among Anglo-Catholics. Then there are the Nonconformist congregations where every child addressed every adult woman as 'Aunty'.[32] I have not done enough work on the place of aunts and uncles in Christian theology.

The forgiving mother

Nor have I done enough work on the place of mothers. When I read Mrs Sherwood I did notice that the human (meaning humane) voice was, almost entirely, the voice of the mother. As Mrs Sherwood's theology became more liberal, the character Mr Fairchild almost faded away in the two later volumes of the *History of the Fairchild Family*. There is a scholarly debate on the feminisation of religion in the Victorian age. It would be perhaps unfair to brand the young Mrs Sherwood, an example of the old theology, as therefore a mannish thinker. Nevertheless, the new theology could be seen as feminised. When male theologians, later in the century, tried to understand how Christ could bear our sins, they thought of their mothers. I return to R.C. Moberly.

> I will ask you to think of a father, or a mother – pure, holy, tender, loving-hearted – whose own beloved only child, son or daughter, is branded with the deep reality of irretrievable disgrace ...

towards the stranger there might be the deepest concern, the tenderest, truest, most winning and restorative sympathy. But the shame, which is her own child's, is her own. *For herself,* the light is gone out of her life. Her heart is not merely . . . tenderly concerned. Her heart is broken.

. . . compare this grief of the mother with the grief of the child, whose own the shame is . . . The penitence of the child may be fiercer and wilder; but it is, in comparison, shallow, mixed, impotent, unreal . . . The child's heart is less likely to break. The true realisation of shame, the true steady insight into sin, is dulled, not sharpened, by the indwelling of sin . . .

[The mother's] power of penitence, that is penitence indeed, depends not upon the extent to which the guilt is her own, but rather upon the extent to which it is not . . . perhaps there is no other relation, in human experience, which enables us equally to realise how far unselfishness can go towards the self-identifying of one person with another in the unity of nature and love.[33]

Now there, seriously, are Victorian family values. When we think of how 'it would kill your mother' we realise something of what it means that Christ died for our sins, because he loved us.

My first reading is the serious one. I am genuinely moved by that passage. But there are other readings. One side of me says 'This is emotional blackmail'. Another side wants to send it up. I feel like saying to you: 'We shall now sing No 776 in *Sacred Songs and Solos* "Where is my wand'ring boy tonight?".' It may be unfortunate, but we cannot simply respond with simple acceptance to Victorian family values.

There is a great deal that is not dealt with in this paper. I have tried to stick to family values, and so have avoided family facts. Victorian theology was rather fond of contrasting facts and values. As a thought-out system, this is called Ritschlianism, from the German theologian, Albrecht Ritschl. Behind him is the great philosopher Kant. Perhaps science would look after facts, and religion look after values. There were risks in this. Victorian talk is very heavily value-laden – they loved moral seriousness and fervour. Their descendants, embarrassed by fervour, too conscious of irony, saw the contrast between the hard facts of Victorian society and the values it cherished, and spoke of hypocrisy. There is some truth in this, but we underestimate the Victorians' own harsh judgements on themselves. The family values of the Victorian age were there because of sin. We are accustomed, in this century, to over-sweet images of family life, 'God, momma, and apple pie'. Victorian images tied in with a theology of enduring and redeeming love. They were a way of coping with breakdown and defeat. A mother is the image of God.

NOTES

1. I owe the idea of turning to Mrs Sherwood, of whom I knew nothing, to Donald Mackay, a research team in himself, and a tremendous loss to our department. Writers on Mrs Sherwood whose books I used included Naomi Royde Smith, *The State of Mind of Mrs Sherwood* (London, Macmillan; 1946); M. Nancy Cutt, *Mrs Sherwood and her Books for Children* (London, OUP; 1974); Patricia Demers 'Mrs Sherwood and Hesba Stretton: the Letter and the Spirit of Evangelical Writing of and for Children' in James H. McGavran, Jr, *Romanticism and Children's Literature in Nineteenth-Century England* (Athens, GA, University of Georgia Press; 1991). I also used the old *Life and Times of Mrs Sherwood* edited by F.J. Harvey Darton (London, Wells Gardner; 1910).

2. Page references are to the 1879 edition.

3. ibid. p. 41

4. ibid. p. 106

5. ibid. p. 31

6. ibid. p. 188

7. For a survey of changes in later editions, including a charming Edwardian illustration, see Nancy Cutt, op.cit. pp. 76–81.

8. *History of the Fairchild Family* (London, Ward Lock; 1879) p. 22.

9. ibid. pp. 139–163

10. She was criticised by a Miss Rigby in the *Quarterly Review* (Vol. LXXII, 1843, Article II) for her 'manifold pictures of weak and wicked parents'.

11. op. cit., p. 194

12. 'The Story of Miss Crosby and the Green Silk Bonnets' is the first story of Volume 2 of the *History of the Fairchild Family*.

13. J. McLeod Campbell, *The Nature of the Atonement* (Cambridge, Macmillan; 1856), p. 345.

14. ibid. p. 342

15. ibid. p. 337

16. Noel Annan, 'The intellectual aristocracy', in John H. Plumb (ed.), *Studies in Social History: a tribute to G.M. Trevelyan* (London, Longmans; 1955) pp. 243–287.

17. R.C. Moberly, *Atonement and Personality* (London, John Murray; [1900] 1924), pp. 64–5.

18 *Charles Kingsley: His Letters and Memories of His Life* edited by his wife (London, Kegan Paul Trench and Co; 1883), p. 76

19. ibid. pp. 189–90

20. Samuel Butler, *The Way of All Flesh* (Harmondsworth, Penguin; 1966) p. 125

21. Kingsley, op.cit., p. 76

22. Ira D. Sankey, *Sacred Songs and Solos*, No. 852.

23. In her *Life and Times* she tells of how César Malan, the reviver of Genevan Protestantism, 'objected to a passage in the Catechism stories in which I had asserted that Christ, instead of acting according to the will of the Father, had as it were, by interposing Himself between the Father and the sinner, compelled Him to have mercy' (467).

24. J. McLeod Campbell, op.cit., p. 364

25. F.D. Maurcie, *The Church a Family* (London, Parker; 1850) p. 65

26. ibid. p. 117

27. ibid. p. 96

28. W.G. Blaikie, *The Family: its Scriptural Ideal and its Modern Assailants* (1888). There is a large extract in *Religion in Victorian Britain: Vol. III: Sources*, edited by James R. Moore (Manchester, Manchester UP; 1988) p. 204.

29. Housing reformers, however, dwelt too avidly on the risk of brother-sister incest in slums.

30. Maurice, op.cit., p. 177

31. ibid. p. 162

32. Clyde Binfield, 'A Working Memorial? The Encasing of Paisley's Baptists' in W.M. Jacob and Nigel Yates (editors), *Crown and Mitre: Religion and Society in Northern Europe since the Reformation* (Woodbridge, Boydell Press; 1993), p. 196

33. R.C. Moberly, op.cit., pp. 121–4

5

THE FAMILY, RELIGION AND FEMINISM[1]

Grace M. Jantzen

This Christmas, as usual, my partner and I received a great many Christmas cards, some individually, some jointly, and some including her nineteen-year-old Asian son, twenty-three-year-old white daughter, and our two-year-old granddaughter. Some of the cards depicted robins on chimneys, a fat man in a red suit much too tight for him, or groups of people in Victorian costume singing in the snow outside thatch-roofed cottages. But a great many of them featured a white woman and a baby, sometimes on their own, and sometimes with varying and quite remarkable constellations of men. The woman is usually in a costume of blue draperies unlike anything known to historians of women's dress. The sex of the baby is not specified. On those cards where the woman and baby are surrounded by men, one man sometimes seems to stand rather more closely to the woman and child than do the rest, though at other times the attention of the woman and child seems to be taken up by a man on his knees before them with a shiny object in his hand.

What someone not saturated in western religious mythology would make of all this – let alone of the hominoid creatures flying through the air blowing trumpets – I cannot begin to imagine. For of course I *am* so saturated, and unhesitatingly see all these as portrayals of the 'Holy Family'. I know at once that the white woman in the improbable blue draperies is really a poor Jewish teenager, that the baby is obviously (!) male. And the man closer to them than the others? – Well, perhaps his ambiguous status is appropriate, since as a role model for white western males Joseph has always been rather more ambiguous than Mary has been for women. Yet on reflection, this should perhaps cause more surprise than it does. After all, it happens far more frequently that a man becomes husband and stepfather to his new wife's child than that a woman is simultaneously virgin and mother. Be that as it may, these Christmas cards bring together two dominant themes of Christmas: that Christmas is a religious festival, and that Christmas is a time for families. These two themes are brought together in the endless depictions of the 'Holy Family', where, quite at odds with the little we know about the actual birth of Jesus, the ideology of the white heterosexual nuclear family is relentlessly reinforced and sanctified.

So where are the feminists? Perhaps they are outside the Christmas festivities altogether, having nothing to do with such stereotypical and ideologically saturated portrayals of the family? But that turns out not to be true. Some of our feminist friends have indeed sent us the cards with robins on chimney-pots, and a few sent cartoons deliberately puncturing the piousity of the season. But other feminists are right there inside the cards, trying to reclaim or reinterpret or hold on by their fingernails to some kind of solidarity with the 'Holy Family'. And of course these cards are sent to *us*, to two women who make no secret either of our feminism or of our unconventional family grouping, and are sent, often, by others who like ourselves fall outside the standard depictions of the family: gay and lesbian couples, with or without children, single men or women, again with or without children, elderly people without family, families reconstituted in many varieties after bereavement or divorce. Are feminists against the family? How can we be? – many of us choose to live in them. Are we against religion? – but many of us are religious.

And yet that is obviously not where the matter can rest. For there are many, especially but not only on the religious and political right, who would say that the family forms which feminists choose, and indeed our temerity in supposing that unconventional forms are open to our choice, is itself deeply threatening to 'traditional family values', just as feminist reconceptions of the divine are contrary to true religion. Of course, as soon as such claims are advanced, it is obvious that certain assumptions are being made both about what a 'real family' is, and about what 'true religion' must be. There are many who suppose that these assumptions are beyond dispute, simple common sense. However, what I want to do in this paper is to investigate them more deeply, suggesting that there is a closer correlation than is often thought between conceptions of central religious doctrines and of the family, and that feminist investigation is useful both to deconstruct some aspects of this linkage, and also to offer positive ways forward.

At the same time as the Christmas cards were collecting on our mantelpiece, feminist friends of ours in Boston, Massachusetts, including priests, ministers, and theological students, were offering their time and exposing themselves to considerable harassment and sometimes actual risk escorting women and staff at abortion clinics. More than one doctor has been shot, and several people wounded at such clinics; and a woman who goes to them may find herself accosted by a 'pro-life' lobby trying to persuade her not to proceed with the abortion. Though many people who take a 'pro-life' stance deplore the shootings and distance themselves from the harassment, others have been willing to say that a doctor who performs abortions is a mass murderer, and that killing such a doctor is justifiable homicide. Moreover, these same people, as well as a great many more moderate anti-abortionists, claim the moral and religious high ground. They believe that abortion is contrary to the law of God and a violation of family values, and that their opposition to it is obedience to the divine will. As for the manifest fact that many of the feminists who provide escort services at abortion clinics are religious women, that only goes to show, in the eyes of their opponents, that religious feminists are either deceived or deceivers – perhaps both.

Now, I want to be clear that while most feminists I know and whose work I have read, religious and secular, would oppose a 'pro-life' stance, this should not be taken to mean that we are automatically in favour of abortion. On the contrary: we would defend to the hilt the right of any woman *not* to have an abortion if that is what she chooses. Indeed, feminists are also active in campaigning for better social support systems for single parents, more help for people whose children are mentally or physically disabled, and better sex education and availability of contraceptives, all so that fewer women will find it necessary to seek abortions.[2] Contrary to how feminists are often presented by our opponents, I know of no feminists who think that abortion is an easy option. What we do hold to, however, is that no woman should be forced to gestate, give birth to, raise a child against her will: women should have the right to choose. Feminists are not 'pro-abortion' and certainly not 'anti-life'; we are 'pro-choice.'[3]

I recognize, of course, that there are serious moral and theological and human issues around abortion which I do not enter into here.[4] My point is simply this, that if there is one issue relating to the family where religion and feminism are widely regarded as polar opposites it is the issue of abortion. Yet as with the Christmas cards, appearances can be deceptive. For surely there are a great many religious people who would vigorously reject not only the tactics of the 'pro-life' lobby but also their arguments, and support a woman's right to choose whether or not to bear children, just as feminists do. The caricature of religion and feminism as mortal antagonists slugging it out on the battleground of the family is exactly that: a caricature.

The question of power

Or is it? Before we relax too comfortably into academic liberal tolerance, I suggest that we look again: indeed I shall argue that in relation to the family, religion and feminism are in fact in very deep tension. (I wish to make clear here that when I use 'religion' I refer to the particular religion, Christianity, with which I am most familiar: it would be impertinent of me to speak of any other.) The sticking point is precisely that which is signalled in the division about abortion: women's right to choose. Feminists insist on our right to choose not just whether or not to have babies, but to choose also when, how, and with whom to enter into families, to have a say in how the work and play, responsibilities, fun and finances of those families are distributed – in short, not to be submissive or passive but actively mutual and adult in our relationships. And no matter how much liberal religious people today may wish it were not so, the fact remains that centuries of christendom have enjoined precisely the opposite. The most often applauded words of the white woman in blue draperies on the Christmas cards are the words, 'Behold the handmaiden of the Lord; be it unto me according to your word.' That these words of humility, sub-mission, and service have through centuries been enjoined upon all Christian women, not only in relation to God but also in relation to their husbands whom the Church has treated as the divine representative cannot be wiped away by modern liberal thought. If religion and feminism can come to a fruitful relationship, it will have to be by facing up to this fact, not by pretending it does not exist.

The principle of male domination and female submission is put most forthrightly by spokespersons for the religious right, which is mushrooming in North America and steadily increas-ing in the UK as well. According to their teaching,

> God Almighty created men and women biologically different and with differing needs and roles . . . Scripture declares that God has called the father to be the spiritual leader in his family . . . Good husbands who are godly men are good leaders. Their wives and children want to follow them and be under their protection. The husband is the decision maker . . .[5]

While many liberal Christians would be unlikely to express things in quite this way, and would place greater emphasis on mutuality, I suggest that in practical terms these attitudes of dominance and submission, complete with religious sanctions and, often, a suspicion of feminism, cut much nearer the bone than many of us would like to admit. A little later on I shall show how this is so.

It is this principle of male dominance that feminism chal-lenges, and thus strikes at the heart of 'traditional family values'. Feminists hold that women should not be restricted to bearing and caring for children, nor should men be exempt from caring for the children they help to generate. There have been moder-ate successes for feminists in gaining educational and employ-ment rights for women, so that we are able to enter many of the same jobs and professions as men, even though statistically women are paid less and seldom reach positions of authority. But even such moderate gains are viewed with alarm by some, who see women in the work force as contrary to the demands of God and the family. In the words of an American presidential candidate, complaining of the effects of feminism in the USA,

> What did this do to the family? Twenty-five million children under school age are being dumped into daycare centres . . . Six hundred thousand teenage pregnancies last year – what's happening? Well, the mothers aren't home . . . Divorces mean children are losing their role models; they're not identifying with the proper spouse of the proper sex. You have a rise in homosexuality. You have a rise in teenage delinquencies. You've got a rise in rebellion in schools.[6]

In the view of many on the religious right, all these things are equally pernicious, and all are a part of feminism's attack on the family, directly attributable to the rejection of the principle of male dominance, laid down in divine law.

Now, feminism would be quite glad to accept *some* of these charges. Feminists, of course, are not monolithic, and no doubt some exceptions could be found; but speaking broadly it is true that feminists encourage women to think of ourselves not strictly in terms of home-making and child-rearing. We do encourage and try to empower women to enter education or jobs or professions where they desire to do so, and work to make the working conditions, including prospects of pay and promotion, more equitable. We do urge the provision of day care centres, and of redefined division of labour in the home. Though we would resist the charges of responsibility for teenage pregnancies and rebellion in schools, and I haven't (yet!) heard anyone blame feminism for 'joy riding', many of us do indeed claim that the love, stability, and mutuality of a relationship is out of comparison more important both for the partners and for any children involved than is the legal marital status or indeed the gender of the partners – and child welfare indicators appear to bear out this claim.[7] Contrary to those who hold that families are defined exclusively by blood, marriage or adoption, feminists press for the recognition of multiple forms of families, so that those who choose untraditional forms may be supported rather than undermined in our efforts toward stability for ourselves and our children.

To those on the religious right, all this is of course anathema.

Yet surely it could be argued that, as already noted, there are many religious folk who do not take such narrow views, and who actively support many of these feminist aims: many, indeed, who are religious feminists or pro-feminist men. Surely it is not the case that these people continue to advocate the stereotypes of domination and submission which have characterised so much of Christian history? Surely, indeed, there are great efforts, both personal and theological, at dismantling such ideas, and it is now seen that oppression is demeaning to everyone, oppressor and oppressed. Without wanting to deny this, or minimize its importance, I suggest that the tension between religion and feminism goes deeper, often to unconscious levels, in relation to the family, and that it is in the interests of both religion and feminism to probe more insistently into what quickly turns out to be a very sore point indeed.

One way of doing this is to look more closely at the notion of the ideal family, the family pattern which, though it might not always be attained, is taken as the unproblematic norm, and promoted by church and state alike: feminists have learned to view this ideal family with a large dollop of suspicion. Both religious and secular authorities portray the family as the 'haven in a heartless world,'[8] the place where people can find nourishment and security, physical and emotional. The family is the ideal place for children, and is throughout life the centre, the place where one belongs and where one's identity is rooted. The ideal includes also the optimum composition of the family. There should be a father and a mother who are legally married to one another, and there should be one or more children: a couple isn't really complete until they 'have a family' – that is, have children. (It is worth noting that while having children is what makes a couple into a family, the same is not true about having an older generation about: a couple with children is seen as a family in a way in which a couple with one or more of their parents or elderly relatives is not.) In the ideal family, moreover, the father should be the primary wage earner and take responsibility for the family in the public domain, especially with respect to finances, while the mother should take primary responsibility for the on-going domestic routine and child care. Except in the most traditional circles, both partners can, however, contribute to the other's domain, the woman by having a job outside the home, often part time, and thereby boosting the family finances, and the man by helping with cooking, cleaning, and child care. The children, for their part, are to be secure and happy and preferably bright, moving through the school system into jobs and careers, and in due course marrying and establishing families of their own.

This ideal remains dominant in spite of the fact that statistically such a family constellation makes up only about five percent of households in the UK, which in this respect is not unlike many other western countries.[9] And it must be stressed that the family form just described, and seen (with scant historical justification) as 'traditional', is the form which is seen as ideal or at least as unproblematic. It is of course recognized that not all families measure up to this ideal; but it remains firmly in place for all that. If other forms of family are to be tolerated or accepted, it will be on the grounds that they manage to fulfil the same functions as these traditional families; it is against these that they will be measured and assessed. The family itself – this 'traditional' ideal family – is taken for granted as good, as unproblematic. Any problems that arise, arise out of deviance from this ideal form, not from the form itself, which is therefore to be encouraged by churches and by the state – and even by an Archbishop suggesting that the state might promote it by offering tax concessions to those who comply![10]

Now, I want to explore two things. The first is why it is that feminists should be suspicious of this ideal family. The second is what the religious investment is in promoting this as an ideal. Bringing these two investigations together will reveal the tension between feminism and religion in relation to the family, but will also, I suggest, show some creative ways forward. I begin with some of the grounds for feminist suspicion.

The family in women's experience

It is a simple matter to show that women and men think and feel quite differently about home and family. One way to illustrate this is to ask a mixed group in as neutral a situation as possible to jot down their immediate free associations to the words 'home' and 'family'. In groups I have worked with or heard about, the results exhibit a marked gender division. Men, associating on 'home', tend to jot down such items as 'mother', 'food', 'clean socks', 'warmth', and in general things indicating security and nourishment. Women, by contrast, are very likely to write 'kids', 'washing up', 'cooking', 'cleaning', and in general associations with work. This anecdotal evidence of different perceptions is strengthened by a variety of scholarly surveys. Gillian Rose, for example, has shown how male geographers and social scientists have characterised home and family in romantic terms of security, meaning and intimacy, whereas women scholars have characterised home and family as the primary site of women's oppression.[11] Again, there is some evidence to show that men feel most at ease, and are most in touch with their own identity, when they are at home: when they go out to work or for other reasons, they feel they have to step into a role, a public persona. On the other hand, many women feel most free and most themselves when they can get out. As long as they are at home, their identity is so submerged in serving the needs of the rest of the family that they have no emotional latitude to get in touch with their own needs and feelings.[12] When we recall that many women, upon marriage, lose even their own names and are submerged in their husband's identity, it is not surprising that if they are going to forge some kind of identity for themselves, they will find it necessary that this should be not inside the home but away from it, something quite other.

It becomes increasingly evident that home and family, even in the ideal case, are quite literally different places for women than for men. Moreover, men have a great deal to gain from keeping it so. In 1974, Ann Oakley found that women with young children worked an average of 77 hours per week, including paid work outside the home, whereas their husbands worked just slightly more than half as many hours.[13] Since then, things have probably got worse rather than better. A 1988 study of Dutch domestic and employment patterns showed that women spent on average twenty hours a week more than men on housework and child care, irrespective of whether the men were employed or unemployed outside the home. If the women had a job outside the home, they still spent at least fifteen hours a week more than the men on these tasks.[14] While I do not have comparable statistics for the UK,[15] it is widely accepted that Dutch men do a good deal more housework and child care than do British men; so we may safely suppose that women here carry a vastly disproportionate amount of the workload. Moreover, there is still an assumption that domestic and childrearing tasks come naturally to women in a way that they do not come to men; and that when men do take on some of the domestic responsibilities, they are 'helping' women, doing their wives a favour for which they should be thanked, rather than simply assuming part of a shared duty.[16] Furthermore, child care is something which many men regard as something they can *choose* to do or not, in a way in which few women with children regard child care as a question of choice.

Nor is there any remuneration for such labour: work in the home, disproportionately done by women, is not publicly valued. Of course there is a certain amount of rhetoric about how important it is, but when it comes to actual economic reward, it is work in the public realm that is paid for and that is given rewards of prestige and respect. What happens to the money which the man earns? Often, indeed, a reasonably large amount is given to the woman; but it is given to her in order that she may purchase with it those things which the family needs. Whereas the money which the man has left is seen to be his to spend as he wishes, the money which the woman has is submerged in the needs of the household.[17] In this respect, money is treated in much the same way as the space in the house: it is not at all unusual in middle class families for a man to have a room set apart for his use, perhaps as a study or workshop, but it is quite unusual for the same to be true for the woman. After all, the whole house is hers, so why would she be designated special rights to some part of it? The net effect, of course, is that she has no space of her own, but is responsible for the cleanliness and order of everyone else's space, just as, often, she has no money of her own, but is responsible for the purchasing for the whole household.

It is obvious that in all of these things, men are the ones who benefit from traditional family relationships, and their gain is at the expense of women. Still, many women marry, stay with their partners, and indeed declare themselves happy in their marriages and domestic arrangements. Since this is the case, surely traditional marriage and family patterns are good for women too? Surely the feminist suspicion of family is misplaced – perhaps appropriate for deviations from the ideal, but not for the ideal itself? In response to this objection I make three observations. First, women are so strongly socialised into seeing our role as centred around marriage, children and domesticity, and very many women want a male sexual partner and children, that it is not at all surprising that most women enter into traditional family arrangements with a good will and invest a great deal of themselves in making their marriages and families satisfying and happy, often with good success. Second, especially after there are children, it may be emotionally and economically disastrous for a woman to leave her marriage, and many women will go to very great lengths to preserve and make something of it. Third, many men, like women, invest a great deal of positive energy into their marriages and families, and take their responsibilities seriously, even if they do not recognize the imbalances addressed above. Where there is genuine effort and positive emotional bonds, many women and men will feel happy about their marriage and family even though women are, in objective terms, working far more hours and experiencing many more restrictions than are men.

Family violence

The glaring omission in all of the discussion so far is the distressing issue of domestic violence. In the National Society for the Prevention of Cruelty to Children's series of chilling posters in the London Underground recently, one of them pictures a child's playpen, empty. The caption reads, 'One in ten murders happens here.' For many children and for many women, home and family is anything but a safe place. It is widely estimated that one in every four or five females is seriously abused, physically or sexually, at some time in our lives, and in the overwhelming number of cases the abuser is not a stranger but a male member of the family: father, step-father, brother, husband, or uncle.[18]

It has also become clear that domestic violence occurs right across the social spectrum and in every Christian denomination. Although it is very common for people to deny that it occurs in any of the circles in which they themselves move – it is always 'out there', 'terrible', but somewhere else – this says more about the way victims are silenced and made invisible than about actual frequency of occurrence.[19]

Feminists have refused to cover over the issue of family violence and abuse, working at it in both theoretical and practical ways, campaigning for the law to recognize marital rape (only recently put on the statute books in the UK and still non-existent in many states of the USA), setting up women's refuges, crisis centres, and counselling services, and also naming the fact that for every abused woman or child there is an abuser, most frequently a male family member.[20] Anyone who retains a romantic idea of the family can be cured of it forever by working for a time in a women's refuge or crisis centre. Feminists are sometimes accused of being anti-family and blamed for exposing the abuse and exploitation of children and women in families. It is obvious, however, that this is as clear a case of 'blaming the messenger' as one could ever find; and the real question must be what the investment is of those who wish rather to have silence kept about these negative and sinister aspects of the family.

Regrettably, in this silence the churches have much to answer for. Although there is some indication that ministers and theologians are becoming more aware, there are still far too many accounts of abused women and children who never dare to speak of their experiences to their church or minister because they feel sure that they will not be believed or understood. Even worse, there are far too many accounts of people who have at last summoned up the courage or desperation to speak to their minister, only to have that minister send them back into the abusive situation with exhortations of patience, humility, and forgiveness toward their abuser.[21] And if this is the case in situations where there is actual violence going on, how much more is it the case where the issue if not overt violence but (merely!) exploitation? What counsel could a woman expect from her minister if she complained that she was working twenty hours a week more than her husband, or that he did not take an equitable share of child care? Indeed, what woman would presume to go to her minister, or look to theological writings, for help with such a problem? And yet, are these not issues of exploitation and oppression? And if they are, how is it that those who purport to speak of a God of justice would have so little to offer in a situation of such pervasive injustice – indeed, by their trivialising of the issue effectively side with the oppressor?

This is not to say that religious leaders take pleasure in the facts of domestic justice, let alone domestic violence. Many of them personally try to make their own relationships and domestic arrangements equitable and mutually satisfying.[22] The point, however, is that at a systemic level family life is regularly a locus of women's exploitation and male domination, and far too often a locus of actual violence; and yet with a few exceptions the silence about this from theologians and religious leaders is deafening, while at the same time they try to promote marriage, the family, and 'traditional family values'. At a practical level far too little is being done by religious leaders to address the injustice; and at the level of theological analysis and reflection, there is very little to make anyone suppose that theologians are interested or concerned.

But this raises the question of *why* it is that religious leaders promote the family without much attention to its pervasive injustices. Why is it that they are not rather bending heaven and earth to try to put things right? I have two, related, responses to this question, the first social and the second theological (and they are not meant to be exhaustive). In the first place, I suggest that religious leaders and theologians have been slow to name and work against the negative aspects of family life because they are themselves to a considerable extent beneficiaries of the unjust system. The vast majority of ministers and theologians are male, and males as a group benefit from the exploitation of females as a group. This can be very hard for them to see, partly because they may have a good deal of investment in not seeing it, but partly also because of a confusion between the individual and the group. In such a situation it is much more comfortable for male ministers and theologians not to become aware of the extent of exploitation and oppression of women in families, and when they do become aware of it, to treat each case as individual, rather than to confront the systemic nature of the injustice.

Theologies of injustice

I suggest, however, that there is a deeper reason for the theological silence, a silence of such magnitude that it amounts to collusion. That reason is this. When once we begin to pull at some of the tangled threads of family life, we find that they are knotted to very central theological doctrines, and if we persist, a great deal of traditional theology unravels. The obvious place to begin is with the teaching that women should be submissive, a teaching reinforced by the woman on the Christmas cards and challenged by the 'pro-choice' activists at abortion clinics. Of course, ministers and theologians who accept as applicable to contemporary domestic arrangements these teachings of female submission and male domination are most unlikely to challenge the exploitation of women in families, seeing the inequalities rather as part of the divine plan. However, although there are still a great, perhaps growing, number of religious leaders who hold this view, my comments are concerned rather with those who would reject it and in principle favour greater mutuality, but still do not address the oppressive nature of family structure as a matter of urgent theological concern. In fact, I suggest that those who advocate the dominance of men and the subordination of women have theological consistency on their side, and that challenging it will entail challenging also a great many other traditional theological assumptions.

This may also be why feminist theologians have written relatively little about the family, except for the area of sexual violence. Really examining the theological underpinnings of the ideology of the family means that central Christian doctrines are brought into question. Feminists who want to remain in their churches have had enough to do in affirming our right to be there, to be ordained and to minister, to be treated as spiritual adults; and have spent much more time on those issues than on issues of family life, which have perhaps been seen as more personal. But here as ever, 'the personal is the political', and feminists, like everyone else, have three choices: refuse to look, leave Christianity altogether, or engage in a radical reformulation of doctrine and practice. It is the third of these alternatives which I am exploring here.

The idea of female submission, after all, does not appear out of thin air, unconnected to a wider picture. That wider picture, already in biblical writings and far more fully in the Christian Platonism which saturated subsequent theological development, took for granted a whole series of interconnected dualisms which ran as a 'conceptual fault line' through Western thought.[23] There was light and dark, right and left, good and evil, male and female, soul and body. In each case the former term was valorised, seen as the positive term, while the latter was seen as inferior, negative. Furthermore, it was always to be desired that the good, the positive, should rule over the inferior: hence light should rule over darkness, soul over body, male over female.[24] Indeed the positive terms were all to be associated with each other, as also were the negative terms: thus maleness was linked with mastery, with mind or soul, and with goodness, while femaleness was linked with the body and the earth, with subordination and with evil. Thus for example it was held that it was far more difficult for a woman to be holy or to achieve sanctity than men, since she had all the extra handicaps of her sex to overcome; and those women who were undeniably holy were designated honorary males.[25] The story of the multiple dualisms running through western theology has often been told. What has not been recognized so often is the extent to which those pervasive dualisms have grounded ideologies legitimating the subordination and exploitation of women by men in families.[26]

Now, Christian theologians increasingly reject some or all of these dualisms and their inter linkage as pernicious, and in tension with such central Christian doctrines as creation, incarnation, and resurrection. A God who creates the world and becomes flesh in Jesus of Nazareth can hardly be a God who sees matter and the body as evil or inferior and to be shunned. Yet male theologians who have recognized this have often failed to acknowledge two crucial points. First, they have failed to emphasise that rejection of such dualisms drives a coach and horses through the ideological justification for male dominance and female subordination. If theologians reject the set of interlocking dualisms as intellectually and morally bankrupt, then they should be doing everything in their power to counteract one of its most oppressive effects. Yet on the whole they have not bothered to do so. Why not?

I suggest that one of the reasons is related to the second point which remains unacknowledged, namely that the capstone and validation of the whole sequence of dualisms in western thinking has been the most fundamental dualism of them all: that between God and the world. Many a theologian who wishes to reject or qualify some of the other dualisms in the interlocking list nevertheless wishes to retain a fundamental distinction between a God who is spirit and the material universe, fearing that the only alternative to such cosmic dualism is a collapse into reductionist materialism. But if such a cosmic dualism is retained, then there is no escaping the implication that the material is inferior to the spiritual after all, and that to become godly is to detach oneself as much as possible from the things of the material world. Given the millennia-old conceptual linkage of maleness with reason, spirit, and the divine 'God the Father', and of femaleness with sexuality and reproduction, the body, and 'mother earth', we arrive back by a very short route to a theological underpinning of male dominance and female subordination, and its endless playing out in family life.

Recovering justice

Theologians who wish to reject this have several alternatives available. One, obviously, is to reject cosmic dualism and affirm instead a holistic understanding of God and the material universe. A central aspect of such a position is a rejection of a reductionist account of matter, thus enabling the recognition that transcendence need not imply something other than matter, but rather revisioning matter itself as alive, analogous to the way that our physical bodies are alive.[27] I have argued elsewhere for such a position, though I did not at that time see the gender implications.[28] I now see that cosmic dualism has for centuries provided an underpinning for the devaluation of women and women's work in reproduction, child care, and domestic labour; and that if theologians do not wish to condone such devaluation the consequences will go to the heart of theological doctrine.

Another alternative which would enable affirmation of the equal dignity of women and men would be to uncouple the linkage between maleness, reason, and divinity on the one hand, and femaleness, the body, and the earth on the other. If such an uncoupling were accomplished, then retention of a cosmic dualism between God and the world need not have the consequences for gender that I have described (though I think that it is still unacceptable on other grounds). But if this alternative is to be pursued, it must be pursued in the face of enormous resistance. It is not enough, after millennia of the linkage enacted in every intellectual and practical sphere, for a theologian simply to say, 'I don't accept the linkage any more,' and suppose they can go on with theological business as usual. It will need systematic, sustained, costly effort of theory and practice to show in detail what it means theologically, and what it means for gender relations, to recognize that men are as fully embodied as women, and therefore are as much responsible for reproduction, child care, and domestic work; and that women are as fully rational as men, and are therefore as capable of decision-making, leadership, and choice. When religious leaders begin to be seen to be making that effort, and not until then, feminists will be able to relax some of our suspicions about religious underpinnings of the destructive aspects of the ideology of the family.

But the uncoupling of maleness and divinity, femaleness and inferiority, goes right across the grain of popular and theological expectation. Anyone who has done even such a small thing as using female pronouns and descriptions for the deity in liturgy – prayed to the Goddess or to Mother God, spoken of God as 'she' – knows how shocking this is to worshippers: sometimes the shock is liberating, but quite often it results in bewilderment, anger, and sometimes threats, obscene phone calls, and hate mail from those who feel it their duty to safeguard the Fatherhood of God. Part of the reason for this is that certain attributes of God, particularly power, are also associated with maleness, so that if God is referred to as 'she', dissonance is generated. Once again, I suggest that this is not innocent, and that it has a direct bearing on the religious ideology under-pinning family life and domestic arrangements.

A simple exercise can make this point better than argument. Take any standard worship material, and make a chart of the terms it uses to address God. If you choose the Alternative Service Book of the Church of England, for example, and examine the collects (the main prayers) for the Christian year, you will find that God is addressed as 'Almighty' more than ninety times, and very frequently as Lord or King, but is addressed as 'merciful', 'compassionate', or 'loving' fewer than ten times. Now if it is the case that prayers both reflect and shape the worshippers' concept of God, then that ratio is worth pondering. It is of course true that the collects occur in a context, which sometimes softens the contours; nevertheless the overall impression is of an overwhelming valorization of power.

Women and the power of God

But should power, even – or especially – absolute power, be worshipped? Should it be seen as divine, indeed as the central attribute of God? Sharon Welch has demonstrated how the idea that power is good, god-like, to be desired and emulated, has contributed to some of the worst atrocities of western history, as men have sought to control and dominate others by force,[29] and in doing so have taken unto themselves the place of God. Her argument concerns such human arrogations of power as Auschwitz and Star Wars; but it is easy to see how it has applied also to domestic arrangements, where men have been seen, and have seen themselves, in a position of domi-nation and legitimate power. Once again it is of course possible to say that this is a complete distortion of the doctrine of divine omnipotence, either because divine power does not mean domination, or because absolute power belongs precisely to *God*, and thus undermines all human claims to power. I myself doubt whether either of these alternative interpretations really works, but that is not the point I want to make. My point, rather, is that if religious leaders do not wish to sanction the arrogation of power by men in domestic situations, then they will have to make that point repeatedly and in detail as a central part of the contemporary theological agenda in discussion of the divine attributes. Anything else, in the face of the long-standing valorisation of power and its appropriation by men, colludes with injustice.

The corollary of the teaching of power as superiority is an acceptance of hierarchy, where men are seen as the legitimate head of the family and the due recipients of its service. Women and children are socialised to accept the authority of the husband and father, and men are socialised to regard the position of leadership and authority as their rightful place – indeed as their duty. In religious terms, women are enjoined to be humble as the handmaiden of the Lord, to offer their service gladly to God and to his designated representative in the family. Again, I am not saying that this is the only way that Christian teaching can be interpreted, but I *am* saying that, given the long history of ecclesiastical hierarchy and its theological interpretations, it is disingenuous for religious leaders simply to say that more subtle and sophisticated accounts can be given and then proceed as though their responsibilities have been met.

But is it not necessary that *someone* take the position of leadership in the family? Are feminists – am I – then advocating that it should be the woman rather than the man? Such questions show how deeply assumptions of hierarchy and patterns of domination and submission have permeated our thinking: why should it be assumed that there must be one person, and always the same one, in charge? Of course if the metaphor of leader and followers is adopted then it will seem plausible that there would be one leader and the rest should follow, though even then there is no reason why leadership could not be taken in turn. But most British families are not on continuous walking trips: the metaphor of leader and followers is not a particularly useful one for the actualities of daily family life. This is one of the areas where lesbian and gay couples and their families have a great contribution to make to religious thinking about families, if only the churches become receptive to the message. For same sex couples the gender stereotypes cannot work, so of necessity as well as by choice we have to learn to develop patterns of mutuality, of partnership based on friendship and trust and reciprocity rather than domination and submission. This is neither to imply that such patterns are automatic or easy for same sex couples, nor that heterosexual couples cannot also develop mutuality; it is, however, to claim that same sex partnerships *have to* find patterns of relationship unlike stereotypical heterosexual patterns, and in doing so are often exploring mutuality and adult reciprocity which could be creative for everybody. It will be a great day for the churches when instead of asking how far to tolerate same sex families they begin to ask instead how we can learn from one another.

Many feminists live in families. Many feminists are religious. But many feminists, even religious feminists, are deeply suspicious of the religious ideology surrounding the family, and are offering alternative ways to think about God, about women and men, about sexuality, and about families. Actually, the people on the Christmas cards I began with might be able to help. After all, Mary wasn't exactly a conventional mother, since her pregnancy was a result of a premarital affair – allegedly with God, no less! Joseph seems not to have had too many hang ups about being the one in control, and even those he did have were kept in check by an angel. And the baby? Well, when he grew up he broke all society's conventions. He didn't marry, he didn't have 2.2 children, he was unemployed, and in some quarters his sexual relations with his male and female followers have been a matter of speculation ever since. What he did teach was generosity, compassion, loyalty, and implacable opposition to oppression and domination of every kind. When the churches base their teaching and practice concerning the family on his example, feminists will be able to let our suspicions begin to melt away.

NOTES

1. I wish to thank my chosen family, Ann, Jill, Elizabeth, and Michael for the insights that ground this paper.

2. Rosalind Pollack Petchesky *Abortion and Women's Choice* (Boston, Northeastern University Press, 1985).

3. Beverly Wildung Harrison *Our Right to Choose: Toward a New Ethic of Abortion* (Boston, Beacon Press, 1983).

4. Cf Harrison; William B. Bondeson et. al. eds. *Abortion and the Status of the Fetus* (Dordrecht, D. Reidel, 1984).

5. Jerry Falwell, quoted by Rebecca E. Klatch *Women of the New Right* (Philadelphia, Temple University Press, 1987) p. 44.

6. Pat Robertson, quoted by Klatch, p. 120.

7. See Patricia Baird, et. al. *Proceed with Care: Final Report of the Royal Commission on New Reproductive Technologies* (Ottawa, Minister of Government Services Canada, 1993) Vol. I p. 456; Laura Benkov *Reinventing the Family* (New York, Crown Publications, 1994).

8. Christopher Lasch *Haven in a Heartless World: The Family Betrayed* (New York, W.W. Norton, 1977).

9. R. Emerson Dobash and Russell P. Dobash *Women, Violence and Social Change* (London, Routledge, 1992) p. 54; Margrit Eichler *Families in Canada Today*. Second Edition (Toronto, Gage Educational Publishing Company, 1988).

10. John Habgood, Archbishop of York, in *The Guardian* 14 February 1995.

11. Gillian Rose *Feminism and Geography: The Limits of Geographical Knowledge* (Cambridge, Polity Press, 1993) pp. 47–56.

12. Y.–F. Tuan 'Space and Place: Humanist Perspective' *Progress in Geography* 6 (1974) p. 201.

13. Ann Oakley *The Sociology of Housework* (London, Martin Robinson, 1974) p. 92; cf Dorothy E. Smith *The Everyday World as Problematic: A Feminist Sociology* (Toronto, University of Toronto Press, 1987).

14. Trudie Knijn 'Social Dilemmas in Images of Motherhood in the Netherlands' *The European Journal of Women's Studies* Vol. 1 No. 2 (Autumn 1994) p. 197.

15. The UK steadfastly refuses to collect such statistics, or even statistics on wife abuse. See Hazel Addy 'Suffering in Silence' in Elaine Graham and Margaret Halsey, eds. *Life Cycles: Women and Pastoral Care* (London, SPCK, 1993) p. 80.

16. Michèle Barrett and Mary McIntosh *The Anti-Social Family*. Second edition (London, Verso, 1991) p. 61.

17. Ibid. pp. 66–70.

18. Richard Gelles and Claire Pedrick Cornell, eds. *International Perspectives on Family Violence* (Lexington, MA D.C. Heath and Co., 1983); R. Emerson Dobash and Russell P. Dobash *Violence Against Wives* (Basingstoke, Macmillan, 1979).

19. Annie Imbens and Ineke Jonker *Christianity and Incest* (Tunbridge Wells, Burns and Oates, 1992) pp. 264–276; Susan Brooks Thistlethwaite 'Every Two Minutes: Battered Women and Feminist Interpretation' in Letty Russell, ed. *Feminist Interpretation of the Bible* (Oxford, Blackwell, 1985) p. 96.

20. Dobash and Dobash 1992.

21. Addy pp. 82–90; Joanne Carlson Brown and Rebecca Parker 'For God So Loved the World?' in Joanne Carlson Brown and Carole R. Bohn, eds. *Christianity, Patriarchy and Abuse: A Feminist Critique* (New York, Pilgrim Press, 1989).

22. However, I do not wish to gloss over the many instances where the minister or theologian is himself an abuser, and where abused women or children are enjoined to silence because speaking out would damage the minister's career. Cf Addy; Imbens and Jonker.

23. Val Plumwood *Feminism and the Mastery of Nature* (London, Routledge, 1993) pp. 47–60.

24. Plumwood p. 47.

25. Grace Jantzen *Power, Gender and Christian Mysticism* (Cambridge, Cambridge University Press, 1995) ch. 2; Margaret Miles *Carnal Knowing* (Beacon Press, Boston, 1989) pp. 53–66.

26. There have of course been wide variations historically in how that subordination has been theorized and enacted. For an account of some of them, see Jean Bethke Elshtain, ed. *The Family in Political Thought* (Amherst, University of Massachusetts Press, 1982).

27. Teresa Brennan *The Interpretation of the Flesh: Freud and Femininity* (London, Routledge, 1992) p. 3.

28. Grace Jantzen *God's World, God's Body* (London, Darton, Longman and Todd, 1984).

29 Sharon Welch *A Feminist Ethic of Risk* (Philadelphia, Fortress Press, 1990).

6

THE FAMILY IN A TECHNOLOGICAL SOCIETY

Jacqui Stewart

The rise of technology over the last two hundred years has transformed the practical features of human life and society. It has also become associated with a new language of public and political debate. We talk about objectivity, empirical observation, efficiency, rates of change, and so on. We welcome new knowledge, new techniques, increased speed, wider application, greater power. In this paper, I am going to concentrate on some selected aspects of the effect of this new language and thinking on the family. I shall offer a critique from a contemporary Christian theological perspective. What I find significant and interesting may well provoke some disagreement; different concepts of the family are so important in present day social and political debate that it would be rather astonishing if there was nothing controversial in my arguments. I hope that such debate will be creative and helpful.

Theology of the family

I shall begin with a brief theological outline. Elsewhere in this book, both Hugh Pyper and Frances Young advert to the ambivalence of the biblical and Early Church traditions toward the family as it was known to them. Alistair Mason exposes the inadequacy of any simplistic account of the much cited Victorian family values. They make it clear that theology cannot absolutize any particular component of family in any of its manifestations in time and place. It is noticeable that despite the importance of religion and family on the political agenda, there has not been much new theology of the family this century. Present public discourse seems to be concentrating on the family as an agent of social order. Good family values are said to prevent young people being disorderly, criminal, or sexually irresponsible. Certainly, traditional Christian teaching would expect the family to have a beneficial effect on children, but it has a much more positive emphasis. To summarise Christianity in a paragraph is impossible, but the basic theme of the New Testament is that humanity is not alone as it faces the myriad problems of its times, but in relation with a God of love; that in Jesus Christ we see this love; that this love is radically for humanity and radically against the ideologies which pervert and damage human beings.

Any attempt at a theology of family has to be based on these themes to be effective. Our relation to God is reflected in the way that we experience family as a gift, that which we did not ourselves initiate, but out of which we come from child to adult, and from which we receive, as adults having children. Family relationships in present secular times are expressed less in this language of gift and more in terms of intersubjective relation between partners.

Such modern descriptions present some problems from a contemporary philosophical standpoint. The idea of the enlightenment self as subject is somewhat tattered. The critiques by Marx, and Freud, Ricoeur's hermeneutic of suspicion and the arguments of the deconstructionists have seen to that. However, some modern philosophers, particularly Charles Davis, have suggested ways forward which have interesting implications for our understanding of family. On the one hand, Habermas suggests that intersubjective communication may be the source of values that the enlightenment located in the self. The family can be seen as the first locus of such communication. On the other hand, the critique of modernity, particularly by Foucault, is interesting because Davis points out Foucault's view of the necessity of relations of power for the maintenance of truth and good. Foucault promotes his idea of 'agonism' as always necessary for humans to be ethical agents; and family is one of the locations in which humans are schooled in relations of power. Davis says of the New Testament promise: 'The divine promise is not made immediately to individuals as individuals. They are events creative of community, and it is through the community they found that hope is mediated to individuals.'[1]

And family is the first, most influential and most enduring experience of community that human beings have in our society. To come back to earth, this all implies a continuing important role for the family. It will be the route by which community or self can have an experience of the possibility of truth, goodness and hope. Such a new definition includes the mutual relation of parents as community and the transmission of a tradition of hope and possibility to children. It gives a new impetus to theology, firstly because Habermas' insistence on the necessity of dialogue with the 'other' for the experience of truth recalls the New Testament promise that the Spirit will remain with the community; we do not have private hot lines to God; we need each other. Secondly, Jesus rejects the disempowering of the individual in an unjust society, and offers instead the hope and promise of the Kingdom of God. Our new understanding of the relations of power in human society should allow us to support the enabling of true humanity in our world, which is part of the ushering in of the Kingdom. The theology of family, then, is basically about truth and power.

The impact of technology

In order to enquire about the relation of the family to the world of technology in which we live, we must first provide an empirical description of family and technology. Our present situation is remarkable because of the relatively recent appearance of industrial technology. In the world of Jane Austen, humans and animals were the only consistent sources of directable power (I exclude water and windmills). By the mid nineteenth century, steam, gas and electricity were in extensive use. Now we are in the nuclear age. The family has also changed substantially over the last two hundred years. Jane Austen is certainly not a definitive guide, but she provides interesting snapshots for our comparisons. I will mention some of the changes that have given us the contemporary family, before going on to define some important features of technology.

The statistics tell us that in 1801, the average number of persons in a family was 4.7 (including the unmarried and childless) and the population totalled 8.8 million. The average number of persons in a household was 5.67 and the number of families was 1.8 million. The number of houses was 1.5 million so that 12% of population were 'surplus' to the houses available). Almost two hundred years later, in 1981, we find that the average number of persons in a household has fallen to 2.7. The population has risen to around 48 million. The number of families is around 18 million and the shortfall of houses is estimated to be about half a million.[2] These figures show a large increase, by a factor of five, in the population, a decrease in average household and family size, the disappearance of live-in servants, a large increase in proportion of households of only one or two persons, and a large reduction in the proportion of persons without housing. Marriage has become more common; at the same time members of the extended family are much less likely to share the household. There are other changes in reproductive patterns; the maternal age at starting and completing a family has reduced by five years or more, and this, coupled with increased life expectancy, contributes to the increase in one or two person households. Divorce and remarriage have become common experiences. The death rate for all age groups, but particularly for children, has reduced substantially since Jane Austen's time. It becomes clear that in some senses, 'family' is a very flexible institution, capable of changing rapidly. The nuclear family of the fifties may be giving way to a new kind of extended family as the remarriage of those with children becomes common, and in some places, to another new kind of extended family with baby, teenage mother, her siblings who are aunts and uncles, often all residing with or near the baby's grandparents.

Over this same time period, the introduction of technology has changed many other features of life, which have clearly had enormous impact on the family. People have become accustomed to life en masse. The experience of work was radically revised with the introduction of factories. Education moved from the dame school or the governess into the large scale institution. Mechanised transport enabled a population mobility which had all kinds of possibilities. Modern medicine has given us a totally different expectation of health and life from our forbears. The mass media has transformed the political process, the transmission of cultural values and much else. Two world wars have profoundly affected society at many levels, not least in their effect on the role of women in Britain. All of these changes are intimately related to the development and introduction of technology, to which I now turn.

Science has been characterised as a search for reliable knowledge of the natural world. The crucial feature of science in our society is that it is seen as true. Technology is not simply applied science; there are too many historical counter examples of technologies arising independently of science, and pieces of science that have never been applied, for anyone to maintain that the relationship between science and technology is straightforward. A helpful description of technology is that of Ravetz, who says that it is the goal directed search for capacity to change in a defined material situation: 'We describe as "technical" problems those where the function to be performed defines the problem itself. The goal of the task is fulfilled, and the problem solved, if and only if, that function can be adequately performed.'[3]

Such a technical solution must depend on some true account of a state of affairs, and when achieved, confers power to cause change. Technology is therefore also about truth and power. Technology has brought undoubted physical benefits to the whole planet. This has resulted in a perception of it as essential to modern society – the economic state of nations is seen to depend on 'the visible triumph of technology based on applied science.'[4] The extension of technological rationality to the natural world is seen as banishing barbarism and the evils of ignorance and helplessness in the face of nature.

However, some have seen technology as harbouring danger. Pollution and accident can be the consequences of applied technology. The railway administrator can assemble trucks without knowing what or who is to be transported in them, or to what fate. Political debate can become an argument about the feasibility of building new motorways, or the manner in which computer education will be effected in schools, without touching on the reasons why either are required. Feminists have queried the gender assumptions that come with the practice and exploitation of technology.

The study of the relations of technology and society is not particularly extensive, given its apparent importance. Sociologists have pointed to the 'defining' character of technology; that is, the limiting or directing effect on human behaviour that the widespread application of certain artefacts can have. For example, the introduction of the mechanical clock into factories revolutionised the attitude of modern society to time and work. Studies have examined the roles of men and women in the design, engineering, production, promotion, management, implementation and use of various technologies.

A relatively small number of commentators have made an important distinction between technology in itself and a growing public and political discourse which is assumed to be 'technological', drawing the basis for its validity from science and technology. Much of my paper will be concerned with the consequences of this. In this context, the theologian Jacques Ellul has put forward a provocative thesis about the manner in which technology has come to be used in the modern state.[5] He argues that a technological world view – 'La technique' – has been adopted in public and political talk, which draws some features from technological methods, and applies them, without foundation or reasonable defence, to the conduct of human affairs. He suggests that there are characteristic features of such technological talk, which are both diagnostic and debatable. I will list them here. There is an assertion of disinterestedness or objectivity. Any espousal of value is explicitly rejected. Argumentation is said to be rational, that is, following a calculational logic. Standardisation or normalisation, increase in speed of execution, increase in capacity or range of effect and mere novelty are all assumed to be good in themselves. Behind all this lies the assumption that the extension of power is always to be desired.

If, as I have claimed, the family plays a central role in the interpersonal communication which gives us our understanding of truth as meaning, value and hope, then we have to ask if the truth claims of such a technological world view are in harmony with the process of the family. If the family is the place where we learn about right relations of power, we have to ask if the technological world view enhances the possibilities of just action.

In this context, I have examined three areas where modern technology seems to impinge on the family, however diffusely defined. They are housing, domestic machinery and mass communication. In the rest of this paper, I will look at the truth claims and power relations promoted by technological thinking in these areas, and raise some theologically based questions about its effects on families and 'the family'.

Housing

The provision of housing in Britain seems to be one of the triumphs of technology. At the beginning of the nineteenth century, one eighth of the population belonged to households which did not have a house to live in. This was reduced to less than one fiftieth of the population by the 1980s. There have been vast improvements in physical living conditions for most people. Jane Austen does not tell us about the underside of Georgian society; Mayhew and Dickens, however polemical, were part of the Victorian drive for improvement, and do describe some of the horrors.

The interwar drive to improve housing conditions had to fight not only the legacy of the nineteenth century, with the vast majority of the urban population living in substandard tenements, but also the increasing need for more, smaller units. Death rates were going down, and family sizes were smaller. The state intervened by establishing the scale of the problem, commissioning expert reports, and subsidising the provision of housing. In 1919, King George V spoke to local authority representatives on the subject.

> The housing of the working classes has always been a question of the greatest social importance ... The first point at which the attack must be delivered is the unhealthy, ugly, overcrowded house in the mean street ... If a healthy race is to be reared, it can be reared only in healthy homes; if drink and crime are to be successfully combated, decent sanitary houses must be provided; if unrest

is to be converted into contentment, the provision of good houses may prove one of the most potent agents in that conversion.[6]

The provision of the new housing stressed inside WCs, baths, larders and improved kitchen facilities, covered fuel stores – what you need to be 'healthy'. On the other hand, the parlour, that had housed the piano, couch, cabinets etc. was made smaller, until it finally disappeared under the onslaught of the 'living room'. In the cities, new flats were built, and the famous Quarry Hill flats in Leeds were planned as the definitive expression of the new housing. In the plans 'particular attention was paid to communal amenities such as gardens and playgrounds, tennis courts, shops, crèches, a community hall, communal laundries and drying rooms'.[7]

But actually, most of these amenities were never built because of cost, and in retrospect can be seen to have been secondary, add-on facilities, separable from the 'essential'. The basic requirement was a separate box for each household, providing 'healthy' facilities. These had lost not only the old parlour, but also the dining room, so that fixed shared spaces for communal activity were being progressively eliminated. We may note here that early feminists wished to encourage the communal dimension of housing; in 1916, Alice Austin, an American feminist architect, drew up plans for a feminist socialist city, with communal facilities for laundry, sewing, preparation and delivery of food, leisure activities etc. It was never built, all though there were small scale experiments in the USA up to the First World War. This era ended in 1931 when the Hoover commission in the USA advocated single family home ownership as a way to house the USA, starting the retreat to the suburbs.[8] In Britain, the use of building technology as opposed to craftsmen builders was essential to the provision of mass housing, as was standardisation. Industrialisation of the production of house components, e.g. roof trusses, ran parallel with the use of designs based on replicating units. These were seen as cost effective responses to a succession of public reports outlining the perceived minimum requirements for basic housing.

The transformation of the sanitary house into a larger, lighter, better equipped and more comfortable home was principally the result of the involvement of the state in the subsidisation of mass housing from 1919 onwards, and the adoption by local authorities of the successively higher standards set by the Tudor Walters, Dudley and Parker Morris committees.[9]

Problems were made acute with the Second World War. Half a million houses were effectively destroyed during the war, and many more made uninhabitable. Hence the immediate post war attempts at a technical fix – for example, prefabs. A more glaring example is the history of high-rise housing. Problems arose because of the lack of success of the post-war rehousing programme in respect of the poorer groups. A socially conservative reaction which led to the abandonment of new towns, tightening of green belts and hostility of the better-off residential areas meant that local authorities had to rehouse the urban poor *in situ*. A small number of very large building companies gave local authorities little choice; tower blocks were promoted by companies (because prefabrication, etc. on uniform plans meant ease of industrial production, high profitability, etc.) so tower blocks were built. The explanations given did not cite these reasons, but used the rhetoric of technological advance.

A large part of the appeal of high rise was based on its claim to newness, to be the product of technical advances in construction, building research and industrial organisation. Although these aspects were constantly emphasised by the construction industry . . . the technological basis of high rise housing was consistently overestimated as a consequence of its real impact on architectural designing and planning technology . . . another . . . reason . . . was the prevalence of an extremely optimistic ethos about technology in post war British society . . . Both decision makers and 'public opinion' were predisposed to accept policies such as high rise embued with the appropriate technological aura.[10]

In fact, higher population densities can be achieved with low-rise, 'neighbourhood' architecture than with tower blocks. As well as difficulties with quality of building materials, standards of quality control and poor design, high rise was more expensive than other kinds of building (local authorities received a government subsidy for high rise) and it was expensive to maintain. The social problems of high rise housing were eventually perceived.

> The only point about high-rise on which there is now a sociological consensus is the markedly unfavourable effects of this form of accommodation for families with children. Life in a high flat may have a particularly damaging effect on young children whose play is restricted and whose development may be inhibited. And the effects on the children's mothers is equally serious.[11]

Slowly, the need for more open descriptions of housing requirements has been attended to. However, despite the obvious success of a small number of show piece developments, most mass housing in Britain today still belongs to the era of the technical fix, meeting minimum physical requirements but little else. The tendency is to independent activity in personal space, particularly for children, with minimum communal space provided. Thus the effect is to reduce interaction within the family in a household, and to make it difficult to bring together family across households. The eminent architect Richard Rogers said in his first Reith lecture (reported in the Independent newspaper, 13 February 95)

> The essential problem is that cities have been viewed in instrumental or consumerist terms. Those responsible for them have tended to see it as their role to design cities to meet private material needs rather than to foster public life . . . City planning world wide is dominated by market forces and short term financial imperatives . . . Not only have such developments eliminated variety of function from our city centres but in this single minded search for profit, we have ignored the needs of the wider community . . . Putting cities back on the political agenda is now fundamental . . . We must put communal objectives centre stage . . . The problem is not with technology but with its application.[12]

Domestic Appliances

Domestic technology, such as laundry equipment, cleaning machinery and technology for food preparation, has an obvious relation to the family. Several feminist authors have concentrated attention on the relation between technology and society in this area. Ruth Schwarz Cowan has suggested that the standard sociological picture of the preindustrial extended family with mother occupied completely in household and heavily overworked is not accurate. She studied the changing role of middle class women and concludes that it is clear that the mother's role is now *more* important; lack of servants means she now fulfils a wide range of duties; fewer services (laundries, food delivery) mean more work in the household; she has fewer people to manage but more manual labour. She has less contact outside the home than her forbears; her role is increasingly privatised. Rather than making household work less emotionally important, producing the perfect meal or decorating the sitting room is now a matter of sensitivity. Schwarz Cowan argues that the women's movement had white, middle class origins because it arose from the proletarianisation of this former managerial class.[13] Domestic technology has not been used to liberate these women.

It is interesting to note that early feminists saw communal, not technological, solutions to the problems of domestic work and women. The American Melusina Fay Pierce, in 1868, suggested that all domestic work should be done in co-operatives of twelve to fifty women, who would charge their husbands for the work done. With such fees, they would create communal premises for cooking, baking, laundry and so on, with staff being hired at commercial wages for this work. She designed appropriate housing for this model, e.g. an apartment house design patented in Chicago in 1903.[14] Similarly communal aims were shared by Alice Austin, already referred to.

Another facet of the impact of domestic machinery relates to a frequently cited feminist perception of technology. Cockburn and Ormrod write: 'There is a persistent feminist concern that by virtue of being the inventors and designers of the technologies that women use, men enhance their domination of women.'[15]

They investigated the domestic microwave in this context. They discovered that so called white goods (microwaves, washing machines etc.) were perceived as less technical than brown goods (video recorders, cameras etc.). White goods perform functions of transforming labour for others while the use of brown goods is satisfying to user in itself. These are connected in the public mind with separate views of the feminine role as sustaining and the masculine role as agency. They concluded that domestic artefacts are gendered, and they give evidence that the process of design, manufacture, advertising and sale all manipulate the gender of a given artefact for the desired purpose. There is an association of values of design, engineering, production and technology with masculinity, and this is reflected in the power hierarchies in the factories – women on the production line, men as managers, and the role of 'interpretative women', the home economists, who are subsidiary to the engineers and designers (who are men). Hence domestic technology can reinforce imbalanced power relations between men and women. They argue:

> Men's doing and making seems more important, effective and far reaching; women's seems less important, repetitive, a matter of provisioning and maintaining. Men's lives seem a project, women's a cycle . . . Agency should serve sustenance, engineering should be directed to a sustainable everyday life, production should facilitate reproduction. Instead, family life is drained by the work place, every day life is exploited and deformed by Technology and the gift of human agency risks becoming an arrogant masculine project of transcendence that owes no responsibility to care.[16]

There are other important aspects of domestic technology which are not so heavily stressed by these authors and which might prove controversial. For instance, the defining characteristics of the microwave militate against family eating in large groups. On one hand, it is very difficult to cook or even heat a meal for four or five in a microwave. On the other hand, it is preferable to a conventional oven when a succession of three or four people want to heat single meals over a period of two or three hours. Jacques Ellul argues that such a tendency to reduce family interaction is negative; Cockburn and Ormrod approve it and refer rather savagely to 'oppressive patriarchal commensalism'.[17] I think that family eating together could be liberative. Interestingly, primary school teachers of my acquaintance say that children suffer when they lack this experience. It is clear that domestic technology is implicated in important issues for the relations of men and women in our society. If the feminist project is irredeemably modernist, there may be conflict between the feminist view of what should be happening and the theologian who is not committed to the absolutizing of any abstract principle. However, the theologian who wants to build community and relationship within the family can certainly make common cause with the older feminists who looked to a community dimension. They can both agree that what is happening is not desirable and is putting strains on people which affect adversely their ability to maintain good relationships in a shared living space.

Television

The last area of technology that I wish to comment on is the use of television in mass communication. The problem about studying the effects of television is finding satisfactory methods. Cause and effect studies rarely give useful results because useful comparisons are not possible. Studies of information transfer reveal that it is very dependent on the experiential framework of the viewer, who frequently does not absorb the message intended by the television journalist, but some other view altogether. Studies of what people do with television are interesting; Lull suggests that it is extensively used in mediating intra family communication, and not always very positively – e.g. reinforcing negative dominance relationships; in indirect, manipulating relationships.[18] Interestingly, despite the continued controversy about television and children's behaviour, there is very little actual research on the family and television.

But for the theologian, the main problem centres on McLuhan's tag: 'the medium is the message'. Again, Jacques Ellul has written extensively on the difficulties of truth and the word – the problem of mass communication and what we know to be true. We have moved from personal experience to mass circulated 'fact', so that we live in the world where the naked Emperor is clothed. What is not circulated in mass communication has no reality. When issues such as 'baby battering' were first raised in the seventies, those concerned had a difficult time establishing their own veracity. Instead of gaining our picture of reality from our own experiences, Ellul argues that we gain it from the images transmitted by the mass media. Insofar as the 'medium is the message', this is not real knowledge about what we apparently see, because we act on what we really know. Ellul argues rather strongly:

> I watch, but necessarily, because of the screen, I remain at a distance. What I see in the street has the same reality as what I see on the screen. When I meet a beggar on the street or one of the unemployed I look at this person in the same superficial and disembodied way that I do at the living skeletons in the third world that the television shows me from time to time.[19]

This is a one way process of information; we are not involved in the experience of true communication which is interpersonal and engages with the other (here Ellul converges on Habermas and Levinas) and which, for the Christian, is empowered by the presence of the Spirit: 'It is normal that men should be separate and strangers, but the Holy Spirit creates communication between them, and enables them to break through this separation . . . The Holy Spirit alone can establish this link with one's neighbour.'[20] (Ellul 1989: pp. 105–6)

Ellul cites Paul on the glossolalia (1 Corinthians 14.1ff.) to illuminate the theological dimension of communication which is not the mere exchange of information, but is part of a creative relationship of love with the other. He argues that a language must be created which is open enough to sustain such communication.

> If language is to be a vehicle for the word and a possible translator of truth, it can only do so as an open language . . . What is admirable about language is . . . precisely the contradiction, conflict and tension between the fixed structures of language . . . and the ability of these exact means to accomplish something that is not at all fixed . . . it must remain susceptible of being newly filled with unexpected content.[21]

His argument against mass communication is that it operates unidirectionally, with images that provide a closed language, reinforcing present idolatries and shutting out the possibility of the radically new and truthful.

Conclusion

To conclude, I have looked, with a theological agenda, at some of the discussion of the interaction of society and technology in the areas of housing, domestic technology and television. I am struck first and most forcibly by the invisibility of children. I included the comments on the effect of high-rise housing on children precisely because any comment of any kind about children is so rare, even in the extensive discussions of the value and role of television. The studies on domestic technology do not attend to children except at causes of domestic work. I have been told that leisure technology, in the form of video games, personal televisions and the like, are rendering children physically invisible, as they remain in bedrooms filled with such artefacts, and 'keep from under their parents feet'. The theologian and the church must defend the children. They are essential to the gift of family. A technologically oriented society which subordinates the children and their needs to the financial and technical pragmatism of present times is only storing up misery and disorder for the future.

Secondly, I find much to reinforce Ellul's argument that the rhetoric of science and technology is being used in contemporary society to hide decisions and debates that are really about values, and that should be conducted in the open. This is made explicit in the analysis of high-rise housing, where decisions were made for financial and political expediency, and passed off as technological. The use of domestic technology provides other examples; the 'gendering' of technology suppresses the debate that needs to take place between men and women about domestic labour in a post industrial society. The massive expansion of television channels that is presently taking place in the UK is being driven by commerce, not by any need or development intrinsic to technology. As a theologian, I question the truth of the technological world view. I think that material, social and spiritual aspects of the family may be damaged by the untruth of technological public discourse.

Thirdly, Ellul's characterisation of technological rhetoric, with its valuing of standardisation, speed, novelty, and extension of power seems to be borne out in all the areas I have looked at. The technological world seems to have power over more and more people in more and more ways. The exercise of this power is radically opposed to the exercise of power in the Kingdom of God, where those who have power enable those who do not, where real change takes place in a real world. The family is a place where parents and children need to develop as individuals; where they need time to nurture relationships; where stability is essential and where humans encounter each other in accepting love. The values of the technological world view seem directly opposed to this.

Finally, I note that Ellul points out that the consequence of excluding open discussion of value is that questions of why? are replaced by questions of how? – It is not even a question of whether the ends justify the means; in the technological world view, there are no ends. Zygmunt Bauman, in a discussion of technology and bureaucracy, agrees with Ellul's analysis.[22] For the theologian, such conclusions are profoundly disturbing. In such a world view, human activity is a pointless rehearsal of technical possibilities. It permits neither meaning nor hope. On the other hand, Ellul argues that for Christians, the divine promise is of both; the reign of God announced by Jesus is, in the here and now, the means by which God also achieves his ends:

> In this situation it is not our instruments and our institutions which count, but ourselves, for it is ourselves who are God's instruments; so far as the church and all its members are God's 'means' they ought to constitute that presence of the 'end' which is characteristic of the Kingdom.[23]

Both Bauman and Ellul see the state as the locus of the problem, and advocate vigorous local democracy and decentralisation of power as the only remedy. Technology in itself is a mixed blessing; it can be used in a practical way to help societies flourish. The immense strides forward in our ability to provide food, a sheltered and safe physical environment, health care, education, and cultural development show how important technology can be in that establishing of the Kingdom which is part of the realised eschatology of the Christian tradition. A Luddite position is untenable for theological as well as empirical reasons. But technology can be perverted from its proper end. It can be used to validate the public rhetoric that Bauman and Ellul argue against. Techno-speak can also define and be used to manipulate mass society on an unprecedented scale, and this applies to the family as much as anything else. The Christian tradition needs to defend the family, not as a useful tool in controlling the masses, but as a source of real truth and power, a manifestation of the community of the Spirit, the Kingdom that is to come.

NOTES

1. Davis, C. *Religion and the Making of Society* (Cambridge, Cambridge University Press; 1994); p. 204.

2. Data from Burnett J. *A Social History of Housing 1815–1985* 2nd ed (London, Methuen; 1986).

3. Ravetz J. *Scientific Knowledge and its Social Problems* 2nd ed (Harmondsworth, Penguin 1973): p. 31.

4. ibid. p. 21.

5. See Ellul, J. *The Technological Society* (New York, Knopf: 1964) and his *Technological Bluff* (Grand Rapids, Eerdmans; 1990).

6. Burnett: p. 219.

7. Burnett: p. 248.

8. Doorly M. (1985) in MacKenzie & Wajcman *The Social Shaping of Technology* pp. 219–222.

9. Burnett op. cit., p. 335.

10. Dunleavy P. *The Politics of Mass Housing in Britain, 1945–75*, (Oxford, Clarendon Press; 1981) p. 103.

11. Dunleavy op.cit. p. 97.

12. *The Independent* 13 February 95.

13. Schwarz-Cowen R. ch 14 in Mackenzie and Wajcman op. cit.

14. Doorly M. op. cit.

15. Cockburn C, Ormrod S *Gender and Technology in the Making* (London, Sage Publications: 1993) p. 13.

16. ibid. p. 174.

17. ibid. pp. 142–143.

18. Lull, J *Inside Family Viewing* (London, Routledge; 1990).

19. Ellul *Technological Bluff*: p. 335.

20. Ellul, J. *The Presence of the Kingdom* [2nd Edn] (Colorado Springs, Helmers and Howard; 1979) pp. 105–106.

21. Ellul, J. *The Humiliation of the Word* (Grand Rapids, Eerdmans; 1985): pp. 263–264.

22. Bauman Z. *Modernity and the Holocaust* (London, Polity Press; 1989).

23. Ellul *Presence of the Kingdom*: p. 65.

7

THE ABUSE OF FAMILY

Alistair McFadyen

I would like to begin by teasing you with a quotation.

> The family [is] a powerhouse, with a dynamism that is both self-generated and self-sustaining under normal conditions. But if we have no families worth the name, . . . then how do we ever begin to speak of the church or religion and social change? For me the family *is* the domestic church. If we speak of a weak church we are invariably speaking of weak families, and, similarly, if we speak of a rotten society we shall be saying something about family life. So I see the family as that which underpins both religion and society.[1]

Perhaps for some this quotation rings alarm bells as it serves to locate me in the current discussion about family. It does rather sound, does it not, like a typical, conservative Christian attack on the 'Godlessness' which some identify as responsible for the decline in churchgoing, of basic 'family values', the rise in criminality, pre- and extra-marital sex, drugs, rock and roll and probably also for the introduction of *Anderson Country* on BBC Radio 4.

Of course, I set up this expectation in order to tease and, in the end, to disappoint – as you may have guessed when I deliberately did not disclose the source and context of my quotation, which I shall return to later. But I do want to notice how easily and carelessly expectations and suspicions are aroused when people talk about family. I have perhaps succeeded in teasing some into believing that I shall be articulating a reactionary defence of basic family values which turns a particular construction of family into an ideology.

On the other hand, my very title may have had the opposite effect. For it is evident that I am going to ground my discussion of family in relation to its failure; indeed, in relation to a situation in which family not only fails, but in which family as a dynamic life-process is highly damaging: the sexual abuse of children by members of their families.

Anyone who had worked that out from the title might well have had the opposite expectation excited than that which I invited by beginning with my quotation. Why? Because the dividing lines in the discussion about family are so sharply drawn that defenders are expected, not only to mount a defence of the nuclear family as the eleventh commandment, but disingenuously to ignore the various fragilities and failures of family which can have highly traumatic and damaging effects on people. So defences of family often appear to be idealising as much as they are ideological. Conversely, anyone who enters the debate by immediately drawing attention to the situations in which family fails is expected to generalise those failures into an all-out attack on family as an inherently corrupt institution and reality.

I have taken the time to explain all of this because I hope that I shall be avoiding the simplifications of standing in either of the two positions I have caricatured. But without giving you some indication that what follows is neither an idealising defence nor an unqualified attack on family, I believed I would be inviting misunderstanding of my intentions from the outset.

Defining abuse

Why do I use a rather clumsy phrase like 'sexual abuse of children in families' and not incest? Incest is too broad a category to use here, since it includes intra-familial sexual interactions between peers, which I think is misleading to categorise as sexual abuse. When children are sexually abused in families there is rather more involved than the breaking of blood ties or social taboos related to biological or social proximity in family. And I wish to focus on the abuse of power, trust and responsibility – that is, the abuse of the very structure, order and processes constitutive of family – which occurs when children are sexually abused by members of the family significantly older than themselves.

The description of sexual abuse of children in families I shall give is, as it can only be, a highly generalised one. The experience is not the same for everyone. But I do believe that I am charting some of the core dynamics and tendencies. I am talking of abuse within families, but a great deal of what I say would also apply to abuse which happens outside of the familial context. That abuse happens in families is one of a number of variables which contribute to the specific experience of abuse.[2] And so it would be quite misleading to suggest that abuse within families is necessarily worse than that outside them.

Let us be clear what we are talking about. What might count as sexual abuse of children in their families? My working classification is: the involvement of children in sexual activity, or their exposure to sexual stimuli, or their use as sexual stimuli by a significantly older member or members of their family.[3] Let us notice before passing on that family is not taken here to be synonymous with household nor identical with nuclear family. So abuse by non-resident members of a family – uncles, aunts and grandparents, for instance – would all be included.

Note also that the abuser does not have to be an adult, but just significantly older than the child. Age-difference is related to other differentials, such as knowledge, understanding and physical strength as well as differences in social power and status which exist in the family structure, its culture and story.[4] And where these differentials are significant, it is impossible for the sexualisation of a familial relationship *not* to be based on and exploitative of them. So even where the child is manoeuvred into articulating consent, the consent cannot be unforced or genuinely informed even if not explicitly coerced, since the relationship is permeated by these differentials. Cousins and older siblings, for example, might exhibit such differentials significantly as well as adults.

Finally, notice the range of behaviour which is included: vaginal and anal intercourse, certainly, but also exposure to pornography or to older family members sexually stimulating themselves or others, exposure to obscene conversation, the taking of photographs for sexual use. Be wary of assuming that there will be a necessary and simple correlation between the form and the effects of abuse. The trauma associated with non-tactile forms of sexual abuse can be as intense and damaging as that associated with those which involve physical contact.

A classification of sexual abuse seeks to define the range of *activity* which falls into its class. We should, however, be wary of defining the total reality of childhood sexual abuse in terms of the activity taking place. For, if we want to understand what the core dynamic is which sexual abuse sets, up, then we would do well to think much more in categories of *relation* than of *act*. What the abuser does to the child is rather more than subject her to this or that *act*.

It is much more helpful to see the basic dynamic of abuse and of damage as primarily related to the distortion of the processes of relation, the effects of which may not stop when the abuse does or when any physical trauma associated with it have healed. They tend not to stop because of what the abuser does (or may otherwise happen) to close the abusive relationship from other relationships. Where the child is prohibited or inhibited from disclosing, or where attempted disclosure is unsuccessful, it is almost inevitable that the distorted relationship will be internalised and sedimented in the form of a distorted identity. Let me unpack this a little.

The pain of secrecy

When children are sexually abused within the structured context of a family, there is a relationship already in existence between themselves and the abuser. That relationship is likely to involve a basic trust in the abuser, not just as a person, but as one who may be looked for authoritatively to define reality, as a guide to good and bad, acceptable and unacceptable behaviour and to the appropriate exercise and limitations of responsibility. There are, of course, also bonds there in the structured relationship between abuser and other members of the family, which the child might easily believe are stronger than those between them and herself – significant when it comes to the judgement of how disclosure is likely to be received.

The structure of the family might well already cut the abusive relationship off from the child's relationship with other family members. The lines of psychological presence, concern and attention might well be stronger between her and the abuser than with other family members prior to the abuse beginning. That generally does apply where the abuser is a parent, since that relationship often already has primary significance as an horizon of authority, loyalty and commitment for the child and may shield itself more easily from others' inspection with the cloak of privacy due to its special significance and authority. Parental abusers therefore often have less work to do to inhibit the possibility of disclosure to other adults.

Where there is already a diminished sense of physical and/ or psychological proximity and involvement between parents and child, the task of the non-parental abuser is made easier and disclosure to parents is less likely. Paradoxically, where those bonds are strong, their very strength may be exploited by the abuser once abuse has taken place, by suggesting the negative effects of disclosure on the parental relationship, the parents or the child him- or herself.

In any case, when children are sexually abused, they are almost invariably enjoined to secrecy (implicitly, if not explicitly). A secret is something withheld from public communication, a reality not to be shared with others. But the social isolation effected by the injunction to secrecy does rather more than prevent her from bringing information to public expression. It is not just her *communication* which is inhibited; it is her processes of understanding, judging, evaluating the information represented by the abuse.

The child may simply be unable to understand what has happened to her, what this means, to comprehend it as abuse. And her access to other frameworks of meaning, and with them the possibility of combining this new information with other information which she does not have, is interdicted. To put it more theologically: transcendence is blocked.

Part of the trauma of childhood sexual abuse is related to the fact that it can be incredibly *confusing* for the child. The abuse may be accompanied by all sorts of rationalisations and explanations concerning the nature, meaning and significance of what is happening: it is all right, it means I love you; I am teaching you what you will need to know; this is your punishment for being such a bad girl; this is happening because you are wicked; this is just a game like any other we play; and so on. Each one of these presents the abuse as normal and acceptable, as based on values and beliefs which are part of a more public world of meaning.

If the abuse is physically painful or if it breeches public norms and values already internalised, then the child is faced with a conflict of claims about what is right and wrong. Even if the child is psychologically developed and settled in identity sufficiently for it to be clear to her that these rationalisations are lies and that this is abuse, then it can still be confusing to be confronted with someone trusted doing this.

In any case, secrecy itself makes abuse confusing. Even for a child who accepts the rationalisations at face value, the injunction to secrecy itself implies that this is not, after all, something good, normal and acceptable. It is something bad and shameful, or else it could withstand public exposure. But with that intimation usually comes another visitor: this is something which the child easily believes that *he* has done; *he* is to fear exposure. Therefore he may feel guilt.

If, furthermore, the abuser has told him that he will bear sole responsibility for the consequences of disclosure, the break-up of family, for instance, the child is given the illusion that the power is now in his hands. It is very hard for him to resist reading that power back into the abusive situation. If I am in control of the secret, then I must have been able to have stopped the abuse from happening; it must have been my fault.

Just at the point where the child has traumatic new information to make sense of and integrate into his sense of himself and his world, he is isolated from the social means for comprehending and interpreting reality, of locating responsibility, of defining good and evil. Transcendence is blocked and he is left with the highly constricting and damaging reality of abuse. How, then, is he going to answer the question, 'why is this happening to me?'

Self-blame

Since the conflicts and confusions attending abuse cannot be resolved through recourse to frameworks of public meaning, they can only be survived by turning them inward in a series of rationalisations in the form of deep-seated, distorted beliefs concerning the child's identity and value ('I am dirty'; 'it is my fault'; 'I let this happen'; 'I am evil' and so on).

This is powerfully enhanced by the way in which all the child's resources for survival not only permit the abuse to carry on, but have the effect of confirming and more deeply embedding its reality. All strategies for psychological survival are also in effect accommodations to the abuse.[5] They have to take abuse as the unalterable base-line against which identity must be worked out.

Anything that the child does to survive (even strategies employed during abuse, such as dissociation), all her own energies which are brought into play in order to create and sustain a meaningful identity in face of the abuse, effect a further concentration and intensification of its damaging power. Yet, as she cannot prevent the abuse and is inhibited from disclosing it to others, that has to be an organisation of identity around the reality of abuse. Abuse thence becomes the prime informant of identity, entering its very core – yet it does so in a hidden and distorting way because it cannot be properly processed. It distorts the deepest structures of personhood and identity, and therefore her whole ecology and economy of relating. This happens most obviously in patterns of revictimization or future abusive behaviour (not necessarily sexual),[6] but also in patterns of heightened empathy and attunement to others' needs to the point of sacrifice of self which arises, not out of an unambiguously positive sense of relation to another, but as a strategy to protect oneself in a situation of felt alienation from others.[7]

In terms of the theme in this book, such distortions in identity are the vehicles whereby the effects of abuse are capable of transmission *through family*. The child's damaged and distorted identity may now become significantly informative in the construction of the identities of a new generation of family. Here is one strong reason why I wish to speak of the sexual abuse of children within families as an abuse *of* family, rather than simply as an incident of abuse which occurs *in* a family. The effects of abuse are such that their effects are rarely confined to a single individual and often threaten to be communicated trans-generationally.

The issue of consent

Having outlined what I take to be the most significant aspects of the core dynamic of the effects of sexual abuse of children within family, I should like to turn to a basic question: why is this *abuse*? If we term this abuse, then what is it abuse of? What is the good reality which this distorts and denies? What is the appropriate standard of reference against which sexual inter-actions and involvement of children with family members significantly older than they is to be judged as abusive?

Almost all of the literature on child sexual abuse, in the end, operates with standards of reference which tend towards a moral or a scientific naturalism.[8] An empirical description of normal physiological or social function or development is sometimes given and then applied with normative force. So if the fallout of abuse is dysfunctional in relation to one of these natural norms of life, then it may be termed abuse. The sup-posed virtue of such scientific naturalism is that it avoids staking claims about the good which depend for their sustenance on a moral basis which might prove contestable, given the cultural contingency of value systems.

Other accounts, however, do take a moral position, although one that generally depends on a variety of moral axiom which is supposed to be universal (i.e., 'natural'), such as the inalienable rights of individuals to be self-determining. Much has rightly been made in this literature of the absence of the possibility of consent, given the disparities in power between abuser and abused. Too often, however, one finds here a norm of genuine relation operating which supposes that will, and therefore iden-tity also, are relationally pure; that we really will and consent to a relation only in conditions in which our willing had been formed outside of the relationship, independently of its power structure.

Quite apart from the specifically Christian and theological difficulties I have with such a view of the will (Augustine was right to wonder how a will suspended in perpetual neutrality above concrete choices for good and evil could possibly be good or a free will), it really fails to do justice to the situation of children. Children very clearly do not enter family on the

basis of an individual identity which has been settled independently elsewhere already. It is a nonsense to try to handle the
place of children in family in terms of rights to exercise freedom
to choose, negotiate or withdraw from the relationship. Focusing on will, defined in this individualistic way, is not, then, a
helpful way of understanding sexual abuse of children, nor of
grasping the reality of family more generally.

True, there are points in the story of a family where the
exercise of will approximates to this understanding: the consent
to marriage is the most obvious example. But, for the most
part, family is a curious mixture of the willed and the given.
We do not choose our families, but that is not to say that they
are simply matters of fate rather than freedom, as if will had
no place in the making and sustaining of family, even as it
is given to us. One need not speak of will in the terms which
are characterised as typically modern, and which tend to
reduce talk of family to talk of consensual relationships – or
marriage.

As soon as we try to articulate what it is we think children
have a right to, we are likely to cross over into the other kind
of naturalism and invent a list of dysfunctions or harms which
one has the right not to be subjected to. It is not that I wish
to dispute the list of things which are harmful or dysfunctional,
and certainly not that I wish anyone to be subjected to them.
But I do want to ask whether it is satisfactory, from the point
of view of belief in the abundant goodness of the Triune God,
to operate such a restricted norm for human flourishing as that
provided by empirical dysfunction or avoidance of pain? Does
this not work, somewhat paradoxically, to constrict the full
reality of the abused person? Does it not undercut the possibility of their seeing themselves (and their being seen and treated
by others) as oriented towards and constituting a richer,
deeper, more abundant reality – to which they are already
related – than may be characterised in this way? If so, then such
a standard of normative reference parallels just that constriction
of the abused child's reality which is encountered in the very
phenomenon of which it speaks and to which it stands opposed.

If abuse risks distorting a much more fundamental and much
more abundant reality than can possibly be conceived of in

such a framework, then abuse would have to be conceived of as more than deviation of physical or social function; more than short or long-term harm in these functional senses; more than deviation from normative patterns; and more also than the abrogation of the right to be in relation only on the basis of one's own consent.

The family abused

It is here that I want to return, at last, to the quotation with which I began.

So who is the speaker? The clue is in the fact that she regards family as the powerhouse, not of social conformity, but of social change. The quotation comes, in fact, from a black South African woman writing to explain the significance of the Crossroads squatter camp in the early 1980s as an act of resistance to apartheid's assault on the black family. She recognises that the destruction of family life is the significant measure of the regime's economic, social and political oppression and destructiveness. Why? Because family can nurture and sustain people in their humanity; it can sustain them in relation to a more expansive range of possibilities and energies than they can have in isolation; and, through such expansiveness, family may be a vehicle for refocusing and directing their individual energy. This is what she means when she refers to the dynamism of family; family as a powerhouse. Where family is destroyed, she asks, how and where are the energies for social change to be focused sufficiently to be effective? Where is the vision and energy of revolution to be nourished?

Her presentation carries the strong implication that what happened in South Africa cannot be adequately understood if it is construed in terms of an abrogation of individuals' rights, or even those of a racial group. It is, rather, as an assault on *family* that apartheid threatened to emasculate a nation. So the policies towards migrant workers and the Group Areas Act which led to Crossroads cannot adequately be handled in individualising terms as the assault on persons who happen to be in families, or as a restriction of their freedom to choose to be in families. The abuse of persons can be only adequately

understood by reference to the abuse of the relational environ-
ments which might sustain and nourish them by mediating a
positive sense of the abundant and inviting goodness of their
own identities in relation to a more transcendent goodness, to
be found through others and in God.

There is a further aspect which she alludes to which is not
illumined by a focus on collections of individuals whose rights
are being abrogated. That is the sense in which the effects of
assaults on and abuse of family threaten to be trans-
generational. When *families* are assailed by pressures which
they find they have not the power or freedom to resist, and
so cannot sustain themselves, then the effects are no longer
confined to the particular members there at the time, but visit
future generations, and it is primarily children who are the focus
of this trans-generational communication of the destruction of
family as well as of the destructive*ness* of particular families.

We might want here to pause to reflect on structural factors
rather closer to home which place pressures on *family*, although
we may be more used to considering their effects on individuals.
Poverty, debt, unemployment and restrictions on welfare
benefits are obvious examples. It is quite disingenuous to
imagine that the stresses and pressures associated with these
factors affect people only as individuals and not the structures
and processes of relation within which they live. I might also
mention the intolerable pressures under which many in our
so-called leisure society now work under and bring home in
various ways.

In relation to these and other assaults on and abuses of
family, we are forced to ask, quite concretely, whether it matters
if families, or family as a sustainable social institution, break
down? Faced with such concrete assaults on family, even those
of us who normally operate a hermeneutic of suspicion against
its ideology can be surprised at our answers. Are we really
prepared to let family go? Are we happy when we see individuals
and societies regarding family merely as excess and disposable
baggage? Or is family something good – though fragile – and
to be protected?

It is quite coherent, I want to note here, to answer affirma-
tively and still to judge that some particular families have

become so irretrievably damaged or damaging that some members need to be protected from them or that they have to come to an end as presently constituted. That families can be pathological does not mean that family is the pathogen. Moreover, affirming the fundamental goodness of family does not imply that family can never be damaged or damaging. Rather, it is only when we have a positive conception of family that we may more adequately begin to appreciate the depths of what happens when family becomes pathological. Let me relate this more concretely to the sexual abuse of children in families so that my general point might be clarified. That children are so abused should not lead to our giving up on family. Family is rather something good which sexual abuse distorts, damages and sometimes destroys. Without a positive conception of family, one cannot adequately grasp the depths of abuse of and in family.

I think at this point I really do need to be clear what I mean by family. I am not trying to defend any *particular* form of family as an abstract and timeless universal. Family is not, as a number of the contributions to this book have amply demonstrated, any one thing. The concrete manifestations of family are culturally and historically varied. Christian faith often takes fright at contingency, as if family can only be supported in a singular form, a divine, once-for-all given.

The theology of family

Why is family – some contingent way of being family – theologically significant? Dr Pyper's paper makes it clear that such a question can only be answered in a way that is true to the Bible if it avoids idolising family. The goodness of family may only properly be articulated by relating it to the work of God in creation and redemption. The call to make and commit oneself to family is penultimate and related to the call of God which it can serve but can also become an obstacle to.

Family, I contend, is theologically significant because it is a structure of creation through which we may be called by God and others into our humanity; a structure in which we are already in touch with an abundant goodness which invites us into an expansiveness in identity and in relationships. In family, we encounter givenness along with freedom; the givenness of responsibilities which arise, not out of our free election but out of our basic situatedness, but which cannot properly be exercised without freedom and will.

Family is unavoidable. We all have families, at least in the minimal form of biological relatedness, since there is a biological basis to human reproduction. But the mechanism of *human* reproduction is not simply biological. Family requires will and committed futurity along with biology, and sometimes will and committed futurity are sufficient to incorporate people into families with which they have no biological connection – marriage and adoption are the most obvious examples of that. In Restoration drama, as in the practices of arranged marriages in some communities well-represented in Leeds, for example, the fact is honoured that a marriage is not merely a commitment made between two individuals as individuals, but between members of two families. And part of what one takes on in a marriage is not just the baggage of family which we take everywhere with us; we can find ourselves – perhaps many years hence – taking responsibility for the family which we have joined – ask anyone who cares for a partner's elderly parent.

Focusing on children in family should render it impossible to think of family on the basis of the settled individuality of the members – on the basis of an individuality taken to be settled independently of relationships. For children especially, family relationships are given, not chosen. It is in relation to this givenness of family that we are first called into responsibility. We are called to *make* family, to take, accept and call to responsibility in and for it. That is the terror of a theological view of family: that it is in this given situation that we are called by God to find and realise our humanity, as we are called also to call others to their humanity. The fullness of humanity which we are called into is praise of the Triune God. The purpose of family is to make and equip us to praise God, which requires a correlation between security and captivation; limitation with overflowing abundance.

What may be distorted, inhibited and interrupted by sexual abuse is the child's capacity for free, open and joyful encounter with herself, others and the world. Abuse threatens a distortion in the fundamental relation to God, and thence to self and others, to reality as a whole. In its worst manifestations, a survivor lives in a state in which nothing may be enjoyed for its own sake because at bottom nothing can be trusted or accepted, only feared or turned to defensive advantage. And so she may lose the power and resources to be truly for herself, for others and for God. Abuse is abuse of capacity for joy or, in theological terms, of praise.

The sexual abuse of children is an abuse of family, since it is a constriction of and resistance to the richness of life before God and others which encapsulates and encloses the child in a highly restrictive and distorting reality. Family is our primary (primal?) network of relationships in which we find ourselves set before others, and in which we are called to find, nurture and sustain life in abundance with others through time and across the generations. We are called, in our most basic and first form of situatedness, to nurture human beings into a life of mutual trust, wonder and joy, of faith, hope and love. Since, however, family will always prove a precarious and fragile achievement, forgiveness is the oxygen by which it breathes.

NOTES

1. Bernadette Mosala, 'Assault on the Family in South Africa' in Diana L. Eck & Devaki Jain, eds, *Speaking of Faith: Cross Cultural Perspectives on Women, Religion and Social Change* (London: the Women's Press, 1986), pp. 46f.

2. Such as: the age-difference between child and abuser; the use of violence; the abuser's sex; the number of abusers; the child's own psychology and belief-systems; the nature and structure of the victim's family – significant even when the abuser is not a a member of the family; the duration of abuse; whether the victim was made also to abuse others; whether the child was abused alone or with others.

3. Statistics as to the incidence of childhood sexual abuse are difficult to gather accurately. However, data from the most reliable research, using classifications similar to the one here suggests that a minimum of 10%, and a possible maximum of around 30%, of all children are sexually abused. In little less than half of these instances, the abuser is a member of the child's family, and in approximately 40% the abuser is known to the child, though unrelated. The majority (80–90%) of victims are girls. Prevalence of sexual abuse among boys may be estimated at something between 3–9%; that amongst girls, between 15–30%. Girls are more likely to be abused alone; boys to be abused with others, usually their sisters by a parent. Boys abused alone are much more likely to be abused outside the family and at a younger age than are boys abused with others or girls abused alone. The perpetrators in at least 90% of incidents are men. Women abuse around 20% of female and 5% of male victims. (But on the possible

under-estimation of both male victims and female abusers, see Matthew Parynik Mendel, *The Male Survivor. The Impact of Sexual Abuse* [Thousand Oaks, CA: Sage; 1995].) Sexually abused boys tend to come from poorer families than abused girls, and to suffer separately inflicted physical abuse as well, a phenomenon which is more marked when the abuse is intrafamilial. In only 8–10% of all incidents is the abuser a stranger. See David Finkelhor, *Child Sexual Abuse* (NY: The Free Press, 1984), pp. 72f., 80f., 163–166, 177; Diana Russell, 'The Incidence and Prevalence of Intra-familial and Extrafamilial Sexual Abuse of Female Children', *Child Abuse and Neglect: The International Journal*, *7* (1983), 133–146; Carol R. Hartman & Ann W. Burgess, 'Sexual Abuse of Children' in Dante Cichetti & Vicki Carlson, eds, *Child Maltreat-ment: Theory and Research on the Causes and Consequences of Child Abuse and Neglect* (Cambridge: CUP, 1989), pp. 98f., 155f.

4. On the significance of the disparities in knowledge and power in relation to the issue of consent, see, e.g., David Finkelhor, *Child Sexual Abuse*, pp. 17–22; Karin C. Meiselman, *Resolving the Trauma of Incest: Reintegration Therapy with Survivors* (San Francisco: Jossey-Bass, 1990), pp. 27, 37; Gay Search, *The Last Taboo: Sexual Abuse of Children* (Harmondsworth, Middx.: Penguin, 1988), pp. 8, 152f.; Emily Driver, 'Introduction' to Emily Driver & Audrey Droisen, eds, *Child Sexual Abuse: Feminist Perspectives* (London: Macmillan, 1989), pp. 4ff.; Cathy Waldby, Atosha Clancy, Jan Emetchi & Caroline Summerfield, 'Theoretical Perspectives on Father-Daughter Incest' ibid., pp. 101–105.

5. Cf. Karin C. Meiselman, *Resolving the Trauma of Incest: Reintegration Therapy with Survivors*, p. 90.

6. This tends to fall out in gender-related patterns, with revictimization more common among women survivors; propensity to become an abuser (not necessarily sexually, and not exclusively of children) more common among men. See: J. Miller, D. Moeller, A. Kaufman, P. DiVasto, D. Pathak & J. Christy, 'Recidivism Among Sex Assault Victims', *American Journal of Psychiatry*, *135* (1978), 1103f.; D. Finkelhor & K. Yllo, *Licenced to Rape: Sexual Violence Against Wives* (New York: Holt, Rinehart, 1985); D. Russell, *Rape in Marriage* (New York: Macmillan, 1982); idem, *Rape, Incest and Sexual Exploitation* (Los Angeles: Sage, 1984). Finkelhor's study in *Child Sexual Abuse* failed to find a statistically significant connection, but offers possible explanations for that – see pp. 193f. On the evidence of sexual abuse in the history of male abusers, see: Finkelhor, *Child Sexual Abuse*, pp. 181ff; and for statistical data, see: M. De Young, *The Sexual Victimization of Children* (Jefferson, NC: McFarland, 1982); P. Gebhard, J. Gagnon, W. Pomeroy & C. Christenson, *Sex Offenders: An Analysis of Types* (New York: Harper & Row, 1965); N.A. Groth, W. Hobson & T. Gary, 'The Child Molester: Clinical Observations' in J. Conte & D. Shore, eds., *Social Work and Child Sexual Abuse* (New York: Haworth, 1982); N.A. Groth & A.W. Burgess, 'Sexual Trauma in the Life-Histories of Rapists and Child Molesters', *Vic-timology*, *4* (1979), 10–16; R. Langevin, L. Handy, H. Hook, D. Day & A. Russon, 'Are Incestuous Fathers Pedophilic and Aggressive?' in R. Langevin, ed., *Erotic Prefer-ence, Gender Identity and Aggression* (New York: Erlbaum Associates, 1983); T. Seghorn & R. Boucher, 'Sexual Abuse in Childhood as a Factor in Sexually Dangerous Criminal Offences' in J. M. Samson, ed., *Childhood and Sexuality*. (Montreal: Editions Vivantes, 1980).

7. In relation to this alienated form of empathy, N.D. Feshbach's findings in relation to the physical abuse of children are undoubtedly transferable to sexual abuse. See his 'The Construct of Empathy and the Phenomenon of Physical Maltreatment of Chil-dren' in Cicchetti & Carlson, eds., *Child Maltreatment*, pp. 349–373. Meiselman, *Resolving the Trauma of Incest*, p. 35, and Emily Driver, 'Through the Looking Glass: Children and the Professionals who treat them,' in Driver & Droisen, eds., *Child Sexual*

Abuse, pp. 112, 116–119, both suggest a gender differentiation in the construction of empathy amongst survivors of sexual abuse. Both empathy and its opposite (abusing others in some way) are regarded as ways of escaping from the sense of isolation, alienation, hopelessness and powerlessness inflicted through abuse, either through a mirroring form of attachment to others' needs, involving a distancing from oneself, or an enacted dissociation or isolation from others' needs in order to enact oneself in one's own power over others.

8. See, e.g. David Finkelhor, *Child Sexual Abuse*, pp. 15–18, 22, 152f. and Jeanne Giovannoni, 'Definitional Issues in Maltreatment' in Cicchetti & Carlson, eds., *Child Maltreatment*, pp. 34f.

8

THE ALLURE OF CHOICE AND THE FORCE OF DESTINY

Gerard Rochford

Most research, thinking, social policy, social work, marriage counselling, family work and psychotherapy takes place in a secular milieu. In this paper I want to think about family relationships from a spiritual perspective. I will reflect upon choice and destiny in family relationships, and upon choice and the technology of choice. I will relate personal destiny and the search for self to our godliness and to God. I will then discuss romantic love, outline a defence of it, and propose that disillusion in human relationships is illusory.

I turn first to choice and destiny in family relationships.

Relationships of Choice

In our society, by and large, we choose our spouse but not our parents and the extent to which we choose our children is becoming more and more subject to technologically based options. It is generally argued that opening up our choices is a good thing. I am not so sure that this is so. It is also a burden.

I am not going to say that choice is a bad thing but I am going to examine the implications of socially approving the extension of freedom of choice, for example into the marriage relationship, beyond the choice of who to marry into the choice of whether to stay married. One of the effects of choice is that it gives rise to uncertainty and anxiety. One of the gifts that marriage bestows is security – the unconditional love which the marriage vows express so comprehensively. Choice entails

118

a sense of loss. Let me give you an example of the burden of choice.

An elderly patient in therapy has been speaking again and again about what to do. She dwells endlessly upon what seem objectively to be trivial choices and recriminations. Then she recalls that up until her seventh birthday her parents always gave her presents which were joyfully received and gave her a sense of being filled with good things. But for her seventh birthday she was taken to a toy shop and asked to choose. The child was faced with a sense of confusion, panic and loss – if she chose one toy she lost the others. Her choice was also experienced as the danger of pleasing one parent while displeasing the other. But the strongest feeling was the most disturbing one of all – greed. She wanted all the toys in the shop. Faced with a world of choice, our primitive selves want everything. Knowing that we cannot have everything we are then faced with a sense of loss. Choice by its very nature is ambivalent. Even when you have chosen, there remains a feeling of dissatisfaction, doubt and the seeds of change.

Many marriages harbour secret yearnings around the love you could have married and gradually sink into the depression of that sense of loss. Such loss is commonly expressed in the words 'they're not the person I married'. Given that the person you did marry may have been very largely a fantasy constructed from your own imperfections which are then projected in their opposite perfection onto your partner, your better half, the statement can be usefully put back by first reflecting – 'were they ever the person you married?' and secondly, 'are you the person *they* married?'.

Those two questions, together with the acknowledged sense of loss, could take many patient and tender hours of therapy or reflection to unravel. They focus upon our sense of our own imperfection, our badness, emptiness and hunger. The partner who feels no longer loved faces the task of searching for someone who will love them, while feeling unlovable. They must search first for their own goodness for it is as if the rejecting spouse has stolen their sense of worth, their sense of self. I will say more about the search for self later.

The prevailing tradition in our society is that we marry the one we love. The marriage vow, whether religious or secular, represents a promise to a monogamous and permanent relationship, for better or worse, for richer and poorer, in sickness and in health, till death do us part. It is clear, simple and everyone making it knows what it means, though none of us, because it binds the future against a necessarily changing reality, know what it entails.

It represents the point at which we choose to close down choices in order to grapple with, enjoy, fear, welcome and resist the unknown against a background of security, the moment at which we move through choice to a sense of destiny – a solemn moment. It is an attempt to recreate as adults the unchosen security of the womb and of infancy and to pass it on to our children, to create a sense of security within which a myriad of choices, and therefore mistakes, can be made in safety.

Between the marriage choices of those who repeat their earlier happiness in their marriage and those who repeat their earlier desolation, for whom the loss which the choice seeks to remedy is too great, lie most of us. And it is there that the choice of partner is sufficiently conscious to succeed yet sufficiently unconscious and unknowable to require the closing down of choice which the vow entails. For this vow to be retractable, as clearly it now is, places upon the spouse the burden of needing to be perfect without the security, which as children we should enjoy, within which to be imperfect without being abandoned. If the vow is retractable the fantasy of the 'perfect other' is sustained (the mental reservation to monogamy). Therapists are often themselves the client's embodiment of the 'perfect other' as are memories of the person you did not marry.

Relationships of Destiny

When working with a couple a therapist is aware that the room is filled with other presences, ghosts, images, memories of others. In particular the couple have with them thoughts and feelings about their parents, their siblings and their children.

When dealing with such feelings we are dealing with love and hate in the context of destiny rather than of choice. We do not choose our family relations and must live there within an unchangeable reality. Even this is sometimes resisted – for example, adolescent fantasies of being an adopted child. These relationships cannot be un-made, however much pain they bring. They are our destiny.

Choice and Destiny in the Family

It seems to me that working for the best relationship against the background of an unchangeable reality is the hardest but also the most poignant discipline of all. The marriage vows, or any commitments to a partner in intimate union, are an attempt to borrow from that discipline and that destiny, to proceed as if the relationship were an unchosen, necessary reality – a vocation, a calling, as indeed it is. It is clear that contemporary marriage and analogous relationships no longer represent the struggle to create and to work with an unchanging reality, even though couples still intend to do so when they commit themselves.

Similarly, the parenting of children is becoming more and more subject to choice rather than a response to unchangeable necessity. We choose the number we have, and we can choose, by the technology of foetal scans and abortion, whether or not to bear boys or girls, babies that come too soon or too late, damaged babies, babies that interfere with our careers, or our affairs. Over 170,000 babies a year are aborted. Spouses rejected in divorce run at about the same number per year.

Could it be that by making spouses and children the objects of continuing choice – and I distinguish here choosing who to marry and whether to conceive, from choosing whether to stay married or bear the child – we place the kind of burdens upon each other which we place upon other chosen and rejectable objects, which if they fail to live up to our expectations, can be dispensed with and/or exchanged?

Ever since Freud, analysts, therapists and counsellors have assumed that adult relationships are best understood in terms of infant-parent relationships. Is this because if you cannot come to live peacefully and creatively within unchosen, necessary relationships, when faced with the possibilities of choice you will be overwhelmed by anxiety, greed, dissatisfaction and loss, as was the child in the toy shop? The marriage vows represent the attempt to save ourselves from limitless and therefore insatiable choice experiences. The irony here is that limitless choice induces a state of compulsion, the sense of being driven rather than of being free.

Yet of course the prospect of choice remains alluring because it sets before us the infinite possibilities of betterment. And contemporary medical and scientific technology, beneficial though it is, is continuously widening and deepening the kind of choices which can be made in the context of family and other intimate relationships. Here are some examples:

We can choose whether or not to conceive, and by whom, and by what methods, and having conceived whether or not to bear the child. We can change the shapes of our noses, our breasts, our eyes, our ears, change our height, our wrinkles, our hairlines. We can chose the time of birth and of death by euthanasia (in some countries) or switching off life support machines. We can chose some degree of sex change by surgery and hormonal interventions. We can buy human sperm, eggs, embryos, rent or borrow wombs, place embryos in post-menopausal wombs, freeze sperm for future use, and freeze our whole bodies in the hope of an earthly resurrection.

It is sometimes said of such technologically based choices that we are playing at God. But is it not the case that one of the most evident and frustrating and bewildering, freeing and indeed challenging experiences is the realisation that God *does not* use power, *does not* intervene, *eschews* omnipotence?

Choices attempt to make life as we want it to be. These interventions, represent a wide and deep range of human dissatisfactions, desires, disappointments, sadnesses, tragedies and obsessions which, for motives ranging from the trivial to the majestic, have removed many human experiences from the arena of destiny and acceptance to that of choice and change and their attendant judgements.

The Self as Destiny

Yet some of these choices are *experienced* as accepting a destiny – for example, those who feel themselves to be a woman trapped in a man's body seek medical help not after weighing the pros and cons of being a man or a woman, but from a profound and frustrated sense that they *are* a woman; woman is their true nature, and like a martyr they are willing to go through suffering to testify to that truth. The varieties of subjective sexual destiny seem to have no limit – I read recently of a woman who felt her true nature was that of a homosexual man. She lives in sexual relationship with two men who also have a sexual relationship with one another. And I watched an interview with a man who insisted that his true sexual and personal destiny was as an amputee and who destroyed his leg to have it removed. He seemed content.

But let me return to, I would guess, for most of us, more familiar territory. I am sure that many of us are familiar with the experience of searching for oneself. It is a quest we pursue more or less unconsciously during adolescence and again later with more awareness, often in middle age. It is perhaps more manifest in women than in men, possibly because they are more societally suppressed than men while remaining more in touch with themselves.

The search for self in therapy is expressed by people saying they do not know who they are, they no longer *know* their parents, they feel false, they feel they are acting, playing a role, wearing a mask, chameleons, and above all, lonely. They are searching for themselves. Now that is a curious idea – searching for yourself. How did you get lost – separated? And what a sense of despair that brings with it. Note that such seekers express this as searching for who they *are* not who they *want* to be. They have a sense of the pre-ordained, necessary person who they really are, something given, the datum of their existence which they are called upon to fulfil.

The Bible is full of people with an unchosen destiny: Mary, Jesus, St John the Baptist, Moses, Abraham, St Paul. And the experience of vocation is familiar today, of being called, and called upon, of being chosen rather than of choosing – the chosen people, joiners, artists, farmers, priests, musicians – in all walks of life from the Dalai Lama to the local midwife. Vocation is usually experienced as a spiritual force.

All of us can ask, who is this person that we really are and when and how do we relate to it in ourselves and in others? For there can be no true relating without some proximity to our *true* natures. But what is our true nature?

I wish to come at this from three places: from a prayer by Rudolph Steiner, from the Catholic Catechism, and from Kierkegaard's *The Sickness Unto Death*.

Faithfulness

Part of my work is to meet with a group of people who serve as counsellors in the Rudolph Steiner Camphill Communities in Aberdeen, which care for disturbed and wounded children and adults. We begin our meetings with the following prayer handed down by Rudolph Steiner.

> Create for yourselves a resolute understanding of faithfulness. What we call faithfulness is so quickly lost. But this you shall make your faithfulness. You will experience in another person, moments, fleeting moments when they appear to you as though filled with the original image of their higher spiritual being. And then there will come long other times when those people darken themselves. But you should learn to say in such times 'the spirit makes me strong. I am thinking of this original image. I saw it once. No illusion, no appearance can take it away from me.' Struggle always for this image which you saw. This struggle is faithfulness. And so striving for faithfulness we will be in communion with one another.[1]
>
> *(based on a translation by Anke Weiss)*

I quote that prayer because what I believe faithfulness holds us to is the glimpse, the vision, the image of God in the other, our true nature. Let me come at this from another place.

When I was a child I was taught the Catechism. I was brought up as a Catholic, and we were taught a series of questions and answers and the catechism, if I remember rightly, began like this:

Who made you?
God made me.
Why did God make you?
God made me to know Him, love Him and serve Him in this world, and to be happy with Him forever in the next.

In whose image and likeness did God make you?
God made me in his own image and likeness.
Is this likeness to God in our body or in your soul?
This likeness to God is chiefly in my soul.

In Steiner's prayer faithfulness holds us to the original, true image of the other. The Catechism reminds us that we are made in the image and likeness of God.

Now Kierkegaard. I have been struggling, mostly without success, to read what he says in *The Sickness Unto Death* and I think I have understood something in it. I think he says that any attempt to dig yourself out of despair arising from the loss of self will place you in even deeper despair unless the search is founded upon the search for the Creator of self; that is, the search for self, (and therefore also the search for another's self) when truly founded, is the search for our relation to God.

To summarise, faithfulness is holding to our experience of the person's true self, that true self is made in the image and likeness of God. The search for the self is the search for our relation to God and to our own godliness.

The Loss of Self – the Search for Self

Psychotherapy means the healing of the soul. What makes the soul sick? Most commonly the loss of relation to the self or to a loved one. Why does this bring such despair? Because it brings with it, we could say it is, a disrelation with God, and certainly with the godliness in us.

Let us look again at how the loss of self is experienced. It is experienced I think most deeply, among the following ways:

There is a sense of loneliness in an ostensibly social life. There is the feeling of not being loved in an ostensibly affectionate life. There is a sense of anger in an apparently calm exterior. There is a sense of being a bad person when others may feel that you are a good person. The common link here is contradiction and disrelation. You are not at home with yourself, or with the self that others seem to see in you. You are not yourself, you have lost yourself, you have lost your sense of oneness. And with that usually comes a sense of having been 'badly served' by your parents.

The most intractable experience of loss of self can be seen in the experience of an abused child who inverts the abuse into the conviction of their own badness. Instead of saying 'my parents are bad because they abuse me', abused children turn the reality into its opposite saying 'Because I am bad my parents abuse me', thus protecting their belief in goodness but at the cost of their own worth. The child's own goodness is locked away in a deep tabernacle of the mind, perhaps never to be unlocked and displayed again. The nature of this abuse and its theological consequences are explored more fully in Al McFadyen's paper in this volume.

More often than not, the feeling of being 'badly served' reflects the distance between a mundane darkened reality and the glimpse of the parent's true nature that the person re-seeking their godliness struggles to grasp more firmly. And if we follow through the idea that the search for self is the search for God, when your true self (or the self of the loved one) is lost, your contact with God is also lost. Those are the sources of existential loneliness, and of the search for love, and of the sense of emptiness in a despairing relationship which seemed once so glorious. Is anything more painful than the loss of love or of being loved?

The search for self and one's destiny is no easier than the path of choices. Even Jesus is depicted as struggling with the task of destiny – praying in the garden in loneliness, feeling abandoned, pleading to be relieved of destiny but finally saying 'not mine but Your will be done'. The person who is seriously searching for themselves is searching for the created self – the self that is in the image and likeness of God. They are seeking to accept their destiny, what was given to them, what was written rather than what was chosen.

It is true this search has many forms, some of which may seem insincere and some which may make us uncomfortable, for example sex changes. But true existential yearning can, I believe, be distinguished from cosmetic yearning. I feel that in cosmetic yearning the goal is to reject rather than accept, to burden oneself with the never satisfied allure of choice in the search for superficial perfection. True existential yearning has a true end and a true beginning – a search for destiny, a desire to keep faith with our created selves. This desire to keep faith with what has been created has, I believe, a powerful expression in other areas of human striving. I will give an example and a metaphor.

Science can be seen as a process of inventing theories of understanding which have no particular status beyond their ability to control and predict the material universe. But science can also be seen as the search for, the discovery of, the revelation of, the nature of the universe which has a truth and a beauty independent of our limited functional vision, but which is occasionally glimpsed and revealed by the blessed genius.

In sculpture we find a metaphor for this release of truth. The sculptor can be seen as releasing the figure from the rock which imprisons it. Consider Michelangelo's series of Pieta's, some finished some barely begun. I find the most moving one of all to be the one where a primitive mother and her son can hardly be discerned, yet with such power do they exist, with such existential yearning strive to be freed to be themselves.

Love

I said at the beginning that the person you marry may be largely a fantasy, an idealised image which makes up for your own imperfection. The words 'fantasy' and 'idealised' suggest an illusion. I would now correct that view by reflecting upon the experience of romantic love. Is it not that when you fall in love you glimpse the true created nature of the other most powerfully, and when you love another person you have an even surer grasp of that true nature? To marry the one you love and to love the one you marry commits us to the task which Rudolph Steiner's prayer enjoins us to – the continuing expression of faithfulness to the created person. For those in arranged marriages the task is no different – to love the one you marry, that is to search for and to relate to the other's true nature, the image of God within them.

Kierkegaard says of the person searching for self: 'By relating to your own self and by willing to be yourself, the self is grounded transparently in the Power which created it.'[2] He describes this formula as the definition of faith.

This can be reformulated in the context of relationships as follows: By relating oneself to the self of another and by willing to know that other self, the relationship is grounded transparently in the Power which constituted the two selves. It is important to note here the balance between willing, and destiny; neither is valued at the expense of the other.

True relating is the spiritual task that marriage, family and other intimate relationships, with all their mundane and harassing detail, sets us. It is also the formula of faithfulness in relationship, and perhaps the meaning of love, to envision and to relate to the godliness in the other, the true light that enlightens every person.

Steiner comes to this too when he says to his students: 'When you practice listening without criticism, even when a completely contradictory opinion is being advanced, when the most "hopeless mistake" is committed before you (perhaps I should have begun with this!) then you learn, little by little, to blend yourself with the being of another and become identified with it. Then you will hear through the words into the soul of the other . . .' Such listening imbues the intimate meeting of two selves with what Winnicott called sacredness.[3] It is the spirit with which a therapist trusts the journey of another through whatever paths they lead one – trust in true yearning.

Now those who are married or in other permanent intimate relationships may sometimes feel, knowing what you now know, that if you had known then what you now know you would never have chosen the partnerships in the first place! So why are we so ambitious? Why do we take so awesome a vow of commitment? We must be mad. Madly in love perhaps. I believe we make such commitments because we have the gift at certain moments and with certain people to perceive, receive, and to be entranced by the other's true created nature – an experience of such impact that we wish to bind ourselves to them forever. The experience of loving another person, far from being an illusion is an insight. It is disillusion which is illusory, for disillusion, or what is commonly called disillusion, is the experience which steals from us the perception of our and the loved one's true nature.

Idealisation of another is commonly seen, perhaps even suspected, as a romantic fantasy. And no doubt sometimes it is. But reflect on those sacred times when it is most in evidence – the idealisation of a new born baby, the idealisation of the person you're in love with, and the idealisation of a person recently dead. Now we may see it differently. At those times we are most in touch with the true created nature of the person – their *godliness*, which is as real as their ordinary humanness, and ours too. These are religious experiences.

Within the family, these moments of enlightenment, of transfiguration, may be of great rarity – perhaps experienced *only* at birth, falling in love and in bereavement – but without these visions the tasks of commitment within the struggles of everyday life would be overwhelming and the very idea of marriage, of parenting and of other life-long commitments would be absurd.

It is a paradox of economy that the family provides us with an intimate arena within which to develop both sexual and non-sexual love and to understand the faithfulness that each demands. So finally it can be said that family relationships and other intimate relations have at their deepest level the self as created in the image and likeness of God. And although the vicissitudes of our lives darken our true nature it can still be glimpsed, and in times of faithfulness both held and offered, like a lover at one with the beloved.

NOTES

1. Steiner, R. *Knowledge of the Higher World* (London, Rudolph Steiner Press; 1969).

2. Kierkegaard, S. *The Sickness Unto Death.* Trans. W. Lowrie (Princeton, Princeton University Press; 1968).

3. Winnicott, D.W. 'The Location of Cultural Experience' in *Playing and Reality* (London, Tavistock Publications: 1971).

9

FAMILY LIFE – SCHOOL OF FAITH?

Haddon Willmer

Peter Bohler told John Wesley to 'preach faith till you have it'. I write on subjects like the family not because I am an expert but because I want to think about matters which are important, even if they are beyond me. Not surprisingly, then, various barely managed questions weave their way through this paper. Two are specially important: What is the relation between family as a managed and managing institutional unit in society and families as people live them? And how does this distinction relate to any theological or faith-based view of the family?

The family and society

Should the family as a social institution be a concern of high priority to religious people and theologians? Often it is and, it would seem, reasonably so. We properly want a good society, where there is justice and order; where people are not going to get gassed on the underground. Such a society cannot be made simply by moralists moralising, police policing, government making laws, media mediating, employers employing. They all operate at too general, impersonal, a level. Making a good safe society requires some instrumentation able to reach the parts they cannot reach. Everyone needs to be touched and shaped and encouraged from birth to death, formed as a sympathetic constructive person, given a constant inward awareness of the coinherence of concrete rights and personal responsibilities, of the healthy blending of challenge, discipline and affirmation. To humanise people continually and profoundly, practices like the family are indispensable.

So concern for overall social order often generates concern

for the family. The father of modern study of the history of the family, Frederic le Play (1806–82), a French engineer, administrator and social reformist, was motivated by a desire to heal social decay, or even to prevent it. Different kinds of family appear in history; study enables us to see which type achieves the best blend of stability and innovation and what conditions and support is needed by the socially useful family.[1] Le Play stands at the head of a broad modern stream of scientific worry about the family, taking it as crucial for the well-being of society.

In modern times, when crime rises, we look to the family both as a unit of explanation and a unit of repair. Much religious teaching goes the same way. We have given our children a devastated moral landscape, says Rabbi Jonathan Sacks, and should not be surprised at the social outcomes – young muggers on the streets. He argues that we should work for the return of the stable family: 'We severally took the family to pieces, and severally we can put it back together again. Rebuilding the socially useful family is a feasible project: there is much that people on their own cannot do, being overridden by powerful forces, but we can affect our children. Over them we have an influence greater than any pop star or politician (p. 36).' Jonathan Sacks emphasises the significance of religious community, tradition and discipline at this point, because it bridges and holds together the personal individual living by which people make particular families, and the renewal of society and culture. His vision implies an accessible harmony between families working through the problems, challenges, processes and accumulating achievements of everyday small-scale life and the general quality of large-scale society. 'A law-abiding society is created by the habits of self-restraint, cultivated in early childhood and reinforced thereafter by the moral signals we send. To put it simply: every law in the heart means one less policeman on the streets.'[2] The family, therefore, is essential to the strength and order of society, which it serves in the essential tasks of caring for children and making the future. It is the basic, indispensable working unit of society, like a brick that can be used, with others, to built larger structures, both load-bearing and space-giving.

The new Catechism of the Catholic Church stretches the Fourth Commandment – 'Honour your father and mother that your days may be long in the land which the Lord your God gives you' – to treat the family within a larger social context.[3] We might notice in passing, in this text from Exodus 20.12, the mention of father *and* mother; and also the linking of family to prosperous life in the land, reminding us of the economics of the working family, which have been too much neglected in these papers. Here, however, I wish to draw attention to the way the Catechism develops the idea of the text. 'God wills that, after him, we should honour our parents to whom we owe life . . . and respect all those whom God, for our good, has vested with his authority.' With this phrasing, the command to honour parents is used as grounds for inculcating respect for authority generally. Such a transition is only possible where the family is sensed to be of a piece with the wider society, and both are read within a predilection for a universal hierarchy of authority from God downwards, incorporating both large-scale society and the family. If the Catechism did not treat family as a social unit which implies and is inescapably linked with larger social structures, the intrusiveness of its determination to express ethical warrant for the Aristotelian or modern state would be obvious. It is, however, highly problematic to use the Decalogue to justify the modern state, since the Ten Commandments were given to a people who lived in families which had escaped from Pharaoh's state and, without the state, in the wilderness, were exposed to the terror of the presence of God on the mountain, with only the man Moses – no imposing State – as a protective or ordering intermediary.

However questionably, the Catechism presents the family as a socially valuable institution in a society with laddered ranks of authority. 'Authority, stability and a life of relationships within the family constitute the foundations for freedom, security and fraternity within society'.[4] Nevertheless, it also distinguishes the family in a special way, honouring it as the original cell of society, with a direct relation with God of a sort which states and other institutions do not have. The principle of subsidiarity means that larger institutions should not usurp the family's prerogatives or interfere in its life.[5] So the duty of civil authority to support and strengthen family is emphasised, not to exploit it for purposes beyond itself and the well-being of its members. Some of the detailed teaching in the Catechism not surprisingly echoes key themes of Catholic social teaching as it has been developed since, including the right to private property (which protects families from the interfering control of outsiders and commits them to being responsible for themselves); but the potentially fruitful insistence that workers must have sufficient wages to support a family decently (a principle violated monstrously, in our society and others) is muted in this section of the Catechism.

The defence of the family is necessary in the face of the palpable vulnerability of families and persons. Insofar as the family is a unit or cell in society, it can be used in projects of social engineering to achieve goals and values beyond itself. Nations at war demand sons (and now also daughters) as sacrificial offerings. What are believed to be good or necessary causes justify disrupting or neglecting families. We know how far this subordination of family to state, politics and inhuman ideologies can go. Rabbi Hugo Gryn recently summarised the meaning of Auschwitz as 'the denial and the perversion of all the Ten Commandments' – Nazi practice interpreted the Fourth Commandment to mean that children should be made 'to watch the humiliation and debasement of their parents' – and parents had children torn from their arms. Families were desecrated.'[6] As a response to what had happened and can happen to families in modern states, the Basic Law of the German Federal Republic (reiterating a point in the constitution of the Weimar Republic) affirmed the basic right of marriage and the family, putting them under the special protection of the state and explicitly recognising the care of children as the natural right of parents, incumbent on them primarily. Even though the family is embedded in the politically ordered society, it must somehow be marked off from its grasp. This commitment, made in the light of our sorry history of not respecting people in families, makes us ask what it is for the state to respect the family. The state must have some idea of the family, some working definition, if it is to make laws and manage resources in the interest of the family. What of family has the state – what ideas is it capable of entertaining? For the state to respect family, the idea of family must have political rhetorical potency and it must be translatable without serious distortion into bureaucratic and legal process. How truly and fully can the family be respected in the languages states work in?

The ways of looking at and dealing with the family I have so far alluded to treat it as an institution or part of the order of society. And already we have seen that faith and theology often works in these terms. If God is concerned for general human well-being and wills on earth such social orders as will enable human flourishing, it is easy to make the family, seen as a social unit or building block, a concern of faith, a socio-theological category and a special responsibility of religious teachers. Already, in this book, there are historical and prescriptive examples of such discourse. No doubt it has its use, but I do not wish to add to it here. I wish to explore another quite different approach to the family, also theological, if not more distinctively so. It involves a language which is less that of social managers and reformers and more that of people who live, somehow or another, in families. This approach has the merit, as well as the difficulty, that it does not bracket out, as unscientific or anecdotal, the family experience of those who speak authoritatively about family. It does not divorce, theoretically, the concept of family, which analysts and moralists use, from particular families. Its idiom is probably more narrative than systematic; it is closer to the Bible than to the dogma and ethics by which churches are managed. In this approach, God is less the ultimate social manager than the One before whom we live lives which can be out of control in a world which is either badly controlled or beyond control.

The family of the heart

When Mary took Jesus to the Temple, the ancient hopeful Simeon said that her child was set for the falling and rising of many in Israel – *and a sword shall pierce your heart also* (Luke 2.34,35). Some years later, the boy Jesus disappeared to hold a seminar with the teachers in the Temple; when his worried parents found him and he told them he must be about his

Father's business, they did not understand, but *Mary kept all these things in her heart* (Luke 2.51). This text is a clue for me about how to think about family, but not because it is an authoritative model, derived from the story of Mary, Mother of God, blessed among women. It is not Mary who grips me, when I read this text, but my own mother, for I remember overhearing her using these words more than once, to reveal and conceal what she was doing with her family experience, when the sword pierced her heart. So I heard the text, full of meaning, long before I could understand much about my mother's life or what Mary's words might mean in their context in Luke's writing. Family takes us into mysterious, even frightening, experience, much of which we cannot share before it is too much for words, both in its joys and its sorrows.

Family has its being in the heart as much as in the household. The two locations are not to be separated but neither are they to be confused. We tend too much to think of the family in terms of what is actually observable, like households. But, as much as being an institutionalised, manageable entity, family is what is kept in the heart, shaped by elusive powers. Family is in the knowledge, memory and hope of relationships, going beyond the local visibility and practices of household. Family does not only come to be in cohabitation. It is a wider network, involving some cohabitation, but not limited to it. Cohabitation in the household may be the sacrament of family, the enabling sign, but the full reality of family goes beyond that, just as God and all goodness is not bound by sacrament.

The heart that 'keeps all these things' is primarily in individual persons and will often draw back into their privacy and loneliness. But what is in the heart is purely private, certainly not anti-familial. Sometimes, the heart is deeply shared. Often it represents what is common. A community has no tradition, no common memory, apart from persons who open their hearts to make public what is in them. Community structures, buildings, landscapes, do indeed preserve or memorialise all that has gone into making them, but without the interpreter whose heart holds or gains insight into the secret of them, these embodiments are dumb.[7] To locate family in the heart is to talk of individuals but not individualistically. So the remembering heart which makes family is not privatised. It will indeed refuse to cast its pearls before swine, resisting media and other intrusion and misappropriation. It is not privatised, however, because remembering expands the heart and takes others into itself, acquiring distinctive identity through experience which is gained in and because of the life shared with and exposed to others. What this heart has in it comes from the family and is fed back to the family. Thereby and in this activity of the heart, the family exists.

Nor should we suppose that by speaking of heart we are fleeing to a haven of romantic evasion, for this is the heart pierced by a sword. Mary's heart was pierced because she accompanied her Son, though he bewildered and distressed her, until she got to the place where she could see him crucified. Family happens where people accompany one another through life. This is one reason why I think it is absurd to discount couples whose children have left home in order to get statistics to show (often for polemic purposes) that the traditional nuclear family is disappearing or ceasing to be a norm. When children leave home, the household changes; but look at the family in the heart: look at the photos on the sideboard, listen to the stories, consider who visits them, who they would wish to have visiting, or who they would prefer not to see – consider who they profess not to be interested in any longer, perhaps because that is the only way to cope with the pain: then the family people have and actually live within will be discovered, not by a body count but by a knowledge of the heart. Often, what is in the heart is a little network of nuclear families, with the fractures and sorrows included.

If family is in the heart as much as in the household, the line between family and neighbours and friends and working relationships is not to be too clearly drawn. Family has fuzzy edges – good families have porous and hospitable fringes; small children and courting children see to that, quite apart from what the adults do in the course of their working and social lives. Once children are educated outside the home and parents lose control of the children's marriages, individual families cannot be sustained as clearly defined units marked off from others in clearly defined relationships. Thus instability is unavoidable in families. They suffer uncertain identities, because it is often not clear who is in family and how they are in it. Most families have conflicts of vision about what this family is, and is for, along with disappointments and struggles for power in the daily business of shaping the family. Sometimes we may suppose we have got control, but then time carries the children and the parents inexorably into unimagined novelties. People grow older and are driven or seduced into strange territory which the old maps, drawn from earlier life experience, do not cover. Instability is written into the bodily temporality of family and its members. It is not in the first place a sign of moral or social failing, a collapse of the moral order of society, but the inevitable natural basis and condition of family, and indeed all human, existence. It is the ground of what is good as well as what is bad about family life.

So, in evoking a sense of the family as in some degree inevitably unintelligible and unmanageable to people as they live it, I am not thinking only of families which are broken, or full of violence, malice and malcommunication. I am thinking of families of the sort that I am grateful to have lived in – families which are perhaps good enough for human flourishing, families which are not out of the ordinary range of working communities. It is in ordinary families that swords pierce hearts. My present problem is that I do not have the language to analyse and describe this kind of family with any precision or scientific assurance. All the language I can find falls away, so that it sounds either more dismal or more complacent than I want to be. Truth and goodness are difficult for human beings, partly because of our tendency to think in terms of simple alternatives, as though everything were either the disasters and scandals of the wicked or the heroic achievements and beautiful perfections of the good. Actual life happens between these easy languages: and Mary has to keep all these things in her heart partly because the delicate elusive truth of them is more important than speech. But even in putting it that way, I have given the wrong impression: the truth of family is delicate and elusive and yet it is also solid lived substance. The heart is the mighty central organ of the body, not the home of ethereal moods and fragile imaginations.

Family has living power to draw us into the unknown where our languages of planning and social management cannot maintain an orderly grip. When parents give children life, or when couples pledge themselves, each to the other, they are not giving a known gift. Accompanying others on their journey through life is often terrifying and bewildering. It is not surprising that people aim to escape: moving from one family to another, or becoming recluses, or disappearing.

Families put people under pressure to face up to this kind of reality, which comes to us through living family persistently. Families do that by making escape difficult: people can run away from family, neglect what is said to be their duty, but they cannot undo their belonging and, in some form, they carry their childhood with them always. Jacob became Jacob-who-has-had-to-run-away-from-home. Running from Esau is necessary, but Esau is hard to forget: hearing his name will always frighten Jacob. Reference back to childhood is hard to avoid, even when it has to be indirect and occluded because the past was so painful and distorted.[8] Some people have a childhood they can hardly if ever admit to: but they are still tied to the submerged inadmissible past, a childhood they never had. It is hard to stop belonging. Divorce never restores virginity: that is how life is.

The talk of the family

Nevertheless, people do not belong to families as limbs belong to the body: for then they would die if cut off and separated. It is not merely possible, it is common practice, for people to leave families, to put distance between themselves and families. Many families hold together only by having internal distance and leaving each other alone.[9] The family allows and survives various sorts of distance and abstention, but it is also home, the circle to which people expect to be able to return and be received even when they have forfeited all right to be accepted. The long-time deserter comes back. Children return to the parental home, after adventures and disasters, almost as though nothing has happened. They expect any hurts from desertion to be absorbed, put in the past, without inquisition. Many return home, without offering anything like the prodigal son's penitence: Father I have sinned against heaven and before you and am no more worthy to be called your son (Luke 15.18). Family is thus the place where people may or may not accept the troublemaker and the returning deserter, but at least they feel some pressure in conscience and in social responsibility to consider accepting or sticking by 'family'. Family is where father and stay-at-home soon will argue seriously about what to do with the returning wastrel, for the obligation to accept is part of the reality of family – whereas all his friends in the far country felt no compunction about deserting him when his money ran out; they forgot him, they did not discuss him as a real issue.

Such discussion – in various verbal and non-verbal languages – is significant as part of the basic *modus operandi* of families. There people pay attention to the complex qualities of relationships as they move from day to day; they judge what is going on now by comparison with past experience, with idealistic dreams, with fears for what could happen if relationships became worse. In families, relationships are intensely and continuously felt and monitored; they impinge on the heart. Sensitivity is high. It is not only the obvious betrayal that hurts, the adulterous desertion, the decamping with all the family funds; there are more subtle hurts where one feels disappointed and profoundly limited by others in the family, even when they are good. Some feel they are giving their life to and for the family and look in vain for any return. This hurt can be cloaked, by acknowledging in unselfish realism that we should not expect too much of someone else, even of parent, spouse or heir. We may admit that other family members should not be expected to redeem our failures or to compensate for our losses in life. But still, underneath, the hurt is there: we would often like to have more from people than we know it is reasonable or right to ask.

Life together, intimacy, closeness, makes people vulnerable to each other. We know much about each other. In a family, we have seen and been seen in ways we would prefer not to be known. Others in the family know what we would prefer to be kept secret: so we ask, 'Can they be trusted?' There is no guarantee that other people can be trusted, even in the family. An ethic for families instructs us to be trustworthy, but the reality of family is that it is a place where we find out that we are vulnerable to betrayal. It is such experience which teaches us the value of trustworthiness; the family ethic, which in some degree may be exemplified practically by the working family, is also sought, defined and argued for in the very same family, when it is experienced as a place where people fail each other. Children, till they have learnt discretion, tact and consideration, inadvertently or with delight expose their parents and siblings to embarrassment, letting strangers know what should be private truth. Families may truly feel surrounded by those they cannot trust; it is such fear which privatises. This sort of awareness lies behind an example Bonhoeffer expounded in his paper on 'Telling the Truth'.

'Every utterance or word lives and has its home in a particular environment. The word in the family is different from the word in business or in public. The word which has come to life in the warmth of personal relationship is frozen to death in the cold air of public existence. The word of command, which has its habitat in public service, would sever the bonds of mutual confidence if spoken in the family. Each word must have its own place and keep to it. It is a consequence of the wide diffusion of the public word through the newspapers and the wireless that the essential character and the limits of the various different words are no longer clearly felt and that, for example, the special character of the personal word is almost totally destroyed. Genuine words are replaced by private chatter. Words no longer possess any weight. There is too much talk. And when the limits of the various words are obliterated, when the words become rootless and homeless, then the word loses the truth, and then indeed there must almost inevitably be lying. When the various orders of life no longer respect one another, words become untrue. For example, a teacher asks a child in front of the class whether it is true that his father often comes home drunk. It is true, but the child denies it. The teacher's question has placed him in a situation for which he is not yet prepared. He feels only that what is taking place is an unjustified interference in the order of the family and that he must oppose it. What goes on in the family is not for the ears of the class in school. The family has its own secret and must preserve it. The teacher has failed to respect the reality of this institution ... The child's answer can indeed be called a lie; yet this lie contains more truth, that is to say, it is more in accordance with reality than would have been the case if the child had betrayed his father's weakness in front of the class.'[10]

Is the family then a conspiracy against truth? Or is this tailoring of speech a recognition of the need for privacy, gentleness, tact? People are specially vulnerable to those who live close to them, those who have known us from before we were born, or who shared the rough processes of growing up. Sometimes this is more than people can cope with – brothers and sisters do not trust each other totally; siblings move away from each other and think it an achievement if they get through a couple of days at Christmas without an explosion. It is not that they hate or have no care for each other; but previous experience of life together has laid up material in their hearts they cannot handle explicitly or often together. Brothers and sisters are immensely important to each other, often bonds are established in the memory and the personality which cannot be broken; but their importance does not have to be – sometimes cannot be – realised in lifelong intimacy. Sometimes the distances family members put between themselves are wide and cruelly brusque. Sometimes, that seems the only way to establish or hold on to identity. Sometimes a brother rejects a sister, quite explicitly, refusing even to correspond at Christmas, in order to establish a distance and gain freedom from the loaded past become unbearable.

The cruelties and pains of ordinary, non-abusive families are considerable and may be thought by some to disqualify family as a worthwhile and good form of life. But it is because there are significant bonds in family that there can be such hurt, such betrayal, such disappointment, such uncertainty about the meaning or value of life together. The good of the family is its seriousness, its truth, rather than its efficiency in making us happy. The keeping heart rather than the light heart is where family rests. This is a hard saying, since we are mostly conditioned to believe that happiness, freedom from pain, is the practical essence of the good and that only the delivery of happiness can justify family. There may be some, who with a good conscience can live as though the truth about their family is in harmony with realised happiness, without a sword that pierces. But such people are lucky rather than normal. They should therefore be very careful about how they write Christmas letters to their friends. It may be that a standard circular letter cannot avoid being a public word (as Bonhoeffer would put it) and so likely to be untrue to the family.

Many Christmas letters are not honest about the family because they present only the cheerful side of the picture, for semi-public consumption. Those we write to at Christmas are in a curious in-between relation: they are friends we want to keep in touch with; we do not want to frustrate their wish to have information about us. But we are not family with them; we are not in a relation where much of our truth is known and obvious to them, or at least guessable, before we say anything. Friendship which is sustained in this way is easily covered by the veils of self-protecting and self-projecting respectability. We are not living a common life day by day when the only body-language between us is a Christmas letter. There is no shared work, no daily mutual vulnerability, interdependence or venture in this relationship. Much time in families and work-places is spent in speculation: what is eating him today? How does she work within herself? What is going on? We ask these questions about people we live with, long before they explain themselves, if they can, or ever will; such speculation is essential to keeping the family or the work team going. Family is where we cannot so easily hide, where we are open to speculative interpretation by other people who have evidence provided by our daily living together. But the relationship made by the Christmas letter is shaped by the information the sender chooses to give. And what the writer chooses to tell is often culturally controlled. There is an expectation that a Christmas letter will present the family in the best light possible, con-cretely supporting the general wish to believe that families are significant because they demonstrate the feasibility of happiness (of some kind). Some people prefer not to write Christmas letters, this year or any year, because they do not want to keep relationships going at the expense of truth – and they feel they have truth which is unshareable by this method. Sharing unhappiness is not decent; especially at Christmas and the New

Year, we do not want to put others into positions where they will feel obliged to relate to our unhappiness – always a costly business.

People do not normally send Christmas letters to their actual family: what they have to share in family is too complex for the conventional cheerful brevity of such letters, which time and again will be exploded by the known reality of family. Some families, indeed, are cooperative conspiracies to sustain the sense of respectable dignity in the father, or the parents or the dynasty. Some unfortunate families have a social or constitutional responsibility to give themselves to that difficult task. But generally such family self-presentation collapses, rarely by exposure of the skeleton in the cupboard, or the body under the patio, but much more by that irony which runs through the most gentle and loving of family relationships. Because people know each other so well, the little word, the allusion to some incident in the family tradition, the raised eyebrow, is enough to curb the pretence that 'ours is a wonderful family'. Rather, such a family has more important things to do within itself than put on a great public show. Truth and love, truth and hard work, come together in this irony, and achieve a certain kind of happiness, a happiness which includes carrying unhappiness in love if not always in hope. The family then does not want to justify or explain itself to the world, in terms of conventional respectabilities. It lives in the truth of its own love, which may make little sense to outsiders.

The school of faith

If the family is not to be judged by its achieving of happiness, but rather lived in as a mode of deepening truth, it confronts us with our moral failures and social incompetencies. The family empirically is not to be explained simply as the moral bedrock of an orderly society; and if it is given the mission of solving social problems, its failure in that mission will have to be taken into account and allowed to alter both our description and our expectation of the family. There is more chance of understanding families truthfully and specifying appropriate prescriptions for them if there is a perspective which takes human living to be a disciplined pilgrimage of faith, directed towards and by the promise of God through struggles with self-knowledge, sin, suffering, responding to the invitation to love as it is embedded in the happy and unhappy surprises of experience. Generally, such a view of the family has almost totally disappeared from our public language. Yet it is still there in many hearts and needs to be publicly recovered.[11]

Part of the difficulty with this approach is that it seems to regard life as a journey towards what is beyond the world: it is otherworldly. But worse, this view is problematic because it sees the business of life as a purifying discipline or a struggle for liberation from sin and evil: it implies a sombre realism about human sin, actual, universal and even original. And finally it is objectionable because it is so positive about everyday domesticity. Although family life necessarily takes us deep into encounter with sin, with the imperfection of life; although it reaches beyond this life to God, which is far better; it nevertheless finds joy in this mediocre mundanity. That, we may tend to think, is demeaning. It is as though the kitchen sink becomes the baptistry, where the washing of salvation happens. Perhaps indeed it does.

> The daily round, the common task
> Will furnish all we ought to ask
> Room to deny ourselves, a road
> That leads us daily nearer God.

Thus John Keble in a tradition opened up by Luther, who gave up one kind of saving discipline in the cloister for the school of faith in marriage and family responsibility.[12]

Family is a school of faith not least because it tests and challenges faith as well as rewards and encourages it. In family life, we are asked whether we have the courage and generosity to go on affirming the worth of human being in actual, present, deeply known persons. Can it be believed that human being is in the image of God or can be recreated after the image of God is a real question, a test of faith when we are taking particular persons seriously. Family experience threatens serious unbelief: through it we not merely doubt theological dogmas, but find it impossible to trust that this creation is good, that life is a gift to be lived with joy, that there is hope of fulfilment at the end of a pilgrimage which takes its way through family living. Thus in family, faith is at stake in the fundamental struggle for humanity.

Family is not a school of faith by training children up, socialising them steadily and reliably into an old Christendom-style society where religion (not necessarily Christian) is part of the self-evident frame of life. Rather, faith is a struggle, where defeat is possible. The family is a real school of faith: it is not a production line, where raw material is put through processes that reliably bring forth the desired product at the end. Real schools are no more than a series of opportunities and stimuli, which have random, unpredictable effects on those who are in them. Schools always let some students down – and are all the more likely to do so when they are understood as production processes. The only way for a school to maximise its success is to take children and students into its confidence, confessing to them that school is a very frail uncertain human process, in a world God has not chosen to organise as a smooth production line; school will be clumsy, it will not always make available just what anyone needs, when they need it; it will, to some extent, hurt and disappoint those who are in it; but, for all that, the argument will go, school is a good way, if not the best way, to get on with living; it is certainly better than truanting; it can however only work for good for those who work with it as it actually is. Children need to be formed from an early period not merely to engage actively in developing themselves, but to understand the shortcomings of the school as typical of the difficulties of life and to be developing resources of spirit and technique to make the best of any situation. It is not only the young who need to learn to acquire and develop such resourcefulness. Love means being patient, tolerant, slow to take offence, not insisting on rights, trying to be helpful, being willing to keep a poor show on the road, loyal and even courageous in suffering. Children need to be learning the truth of the human world as early as possible in school and family: and of course that is better done by stories of courage and sacrifice and by sharing in the practice of social inventiveness than by lectures in abstract morality.

The family is unintelligible without faith; faith is unintelligible if detached from the human struggle for humanity. Here is ordeal, the falling and rising of persons, the piercing sword and the heart holding and valuing a distinct, accumulating experience. All this goes on all the time, though we mostly have no language for it.

NOTES

1. P. Laslett *Household and Family in Past Time* (Cambridge, Cambridge University Press; 1972) p. 16.

2. Jonathan Sacks *Faith in the Future* (London, Darton Longman and Todd; 1995) p. 36. Also p. 28: 'No society can survive the breakdown of half its families, the vehicles of its journeys across the generations. No society *ought* to survive which provides its children with so little stability, security, attention or love.'

3. *Catechism of the Catholic Church* (London, Geoffrey Chapman; 1994) paras 2207–2257.

4. *Ibid.*, para 2207.

5. *Ibid.*, para 2209.

6. *Guardian* 9 Feb 1995

7. Storm Jameson *The Hidden River* (London, Macmillan, 1955) pp. 233–4.

8. Compare Bernard Kops' new play, *Call in the Night*

9. The Baptist Union *Belonging: a resource for the Christian family* (1994) pp. 27–30.

10. Dietrich Bonhoeffer *Ethics* (London, Fontana; 1964) pp. 367–8

11. Cf. *Catechism of the Catholic Church* para 2223

12. For Luther, see Roland Bainton, *Here I Stand*, (London, Hodder and Stoughton; 1951) ch. 17; H.A. Obermann *Luther: Man between God and the Devil*, (London Fontana 1993) ch. 10.